PEGGY PORSCHEN'S
PRETTY PARTY CAKES

PEGGY PORSCHEN'S

PRETTY PARTY CAKES

sweet and stylish cookies and cakes for all occasions

PHOTOGRAPHY BY GEORGIA GLYNN SMITH

Quadrille

I dedicate this book to my parents, Iris and Helmut,
for giving me support and encouragement
in everything I always wanted to do

Reprinted in 2007 (twice), 2008, 2009, 2010 (twice), 2011, 2012
10 9

This paperback edition first published in 2006
by Quadrille Publishing Limited,
Alhambra House, 27–31 Charing Cross Road,
London WC2H OLS

Editorial Director: Jane O'Shea
Creative Director: Helen Lewis
Editor and Project Manager: Lewis Esson
Photography: Georgia Glynn Smith
Designer: Chalkley Calderwood Pratt

Cataloguing in Publication Data: a record for this book is available
from the British Library

ISBN: 978 184400 307 5

Printed and bound in China

contents

basics

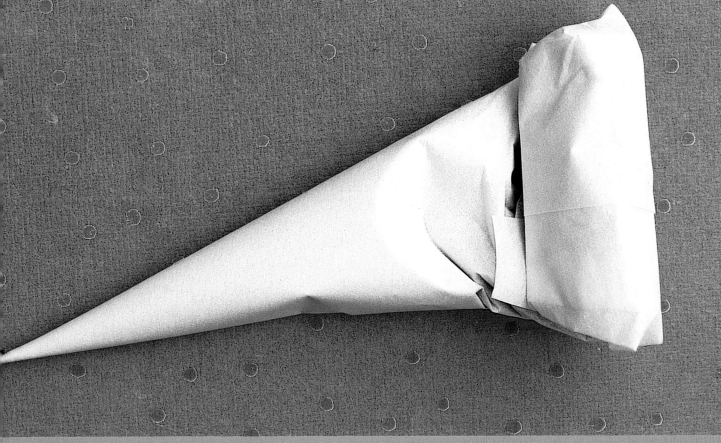

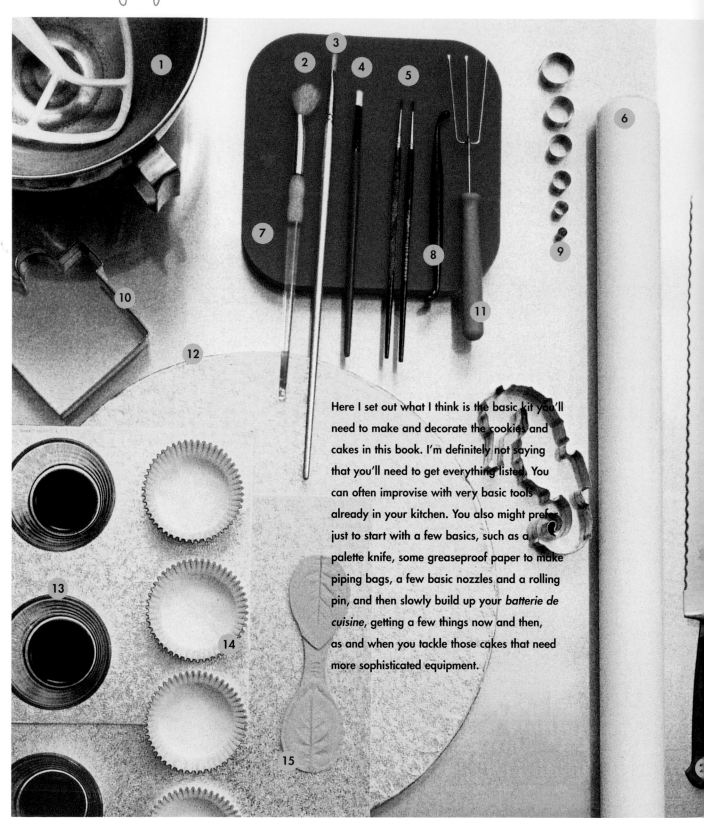

Here I set out what I think is the basic kit you'll need to make and decorate the cookies and cakes in this book. I'm definitely not saying that you'll need to get everything listed. You can often improvise with very basic tools already in your kitchen. You also might prefer just to start with a few basics, such as a palette knife, some greaseproof paper to make piping bags, a few basic nozzles and a rolling pin, and then slowly build up your *batterie de cuisine*, getting a few things now and then, as and when you tackle those cakes that need more sophisticated equipment.

1 Kitchen Aid (metal bowl with paddle attachment)

2-5 artists' paintbrushes (preferably at least 2)

6 large rolling pin

7 foam pad (see page 142)

8 bone tool (see page 142)

9 assorted round cutters

10 various shaped cookie cutters

11 truffle dipping fork

12 cake boards in various shapes and sizes

13 range of food colours

14 paper cases

15 leaf veiner (see page 142)

16 metal side scraper

17 flower nail (see page 142)

18 assorted metal piping nozzles

19 edible glitter in several colours

20 daisy cutter (see page 142)

21 small plastic board

22 large serrated knife

23-4 small, medium and large palette knives

25 lolly sticks

26 small rolling pin

* range of baking trays

* selection of bowls

* wire cooling rack

* baking tins for large cakes

* muffin tray

* large step palette knife (see page 142)

* greaseproof paper

* cellophane

* cardboard

* pencils

* strong scissors

* small needle

* turntable (optional but useful)

* pastry brush

* cake smoothers

* rose calyx cutter (see page 142)

* rose leaf cutter (see page 142)

* ¼ inch (5mm) guide sticks

* plastic dowels

* edible lustre powders in several colours

baking basic cookies eeeeeeeeeeeeeeeeeeeeeeeeeeeeeeeeeeeeeeee

The recipes I have developed give me cookies and cakes that not only taste really nice but have good texture, and – although light — are solid enough to make decent bases for the decoration. Always bake equally sized cookies together to make sure that they cook in the same time. If you mix different sizes, the smaller ones are cooked when the larger ones are still raw in the middle.

BASIC SUGAR COOKIES

MAKES ABOUT 25 MEDIUM-SIZE COOKIES

200g unsalted soft butter

200g caster sugar

1 egg, lightly beaten

400g plain flour, plus more for dusting

OPTIONAL FLAVOURS:

for vanilla cookies, add seeds from
   1 vanilla pod

for lemon cookies, add finely grated
   zest of 1 lemon

for orange cookies, add finely grated
   zest of 1 orange

for chocolate cookies, replace 50g of the
   plain flour with 50g of cocoa powder

EQUIPMENT

✳ **Kitchen Aid or electric mixer with paddle attachment**

✳ **cling film**

✳ **¼ inch (5mm) guide sticks**

✳ **large rolling pin**

✳ **cookie cutters in various shapes**

✳ **small palette knife**

✳ **baking tray**

✳ **greaseproof paper**

✳ **wire cooling rack**

(In a Kitchen Aid or electric mixer with paddle attachment, cream the butter with the sugar and chosen flavouring until well mixed and just creamy in texture. Do not overwork, or the cookies will spread during baking.

2 Beat in the egg until well combined. Add the flour and mix on low speed until a dough forms (see 1). Gather into a ball, wrap in cling film and chill for at least 1 hour.

3 Place the dough on a floured surface and knead briefly. Using two ¼ inch (5mm) guide sticks, roll out to an even thickness (see 2).

4 Use cookie cutters to cut out shapes (see 3) and, using a palette knife, lay on a baking tray lined with greaseproof paper. Chill again for about 30 minutes. Preheat the oven to 180°C, gas 4.

5 Bake for 8–12 minutes, depending on size, until golden-brown at the edges. Let cool on a wire rack.

GINGERBREAD COOKIES

MAKES ABOUT 30 MEDIUM-SIZE COOKIES

200g unsalted butter, diced
1 teaspoon bicarbonate of soda
450g plain flour

for the hot mix:
180g molasses sugar
6 tablespoons clear honey
2 tablespoons orange juice
2 tablespoons ground cinnamon
2 tablespoons ground ginger
1 teaspoon allspice
seeds from 1 vanilla pod
pinch of salt

EQUIPMENT
* deep heavy saucepan
* wooden spoon
* Kitchen Aid or electric mixer with
  paddle attachment
* sieve
* cling film

* large rolling pin
* ¼ inch (5mm) guide sticks
* assorted cookie cutters
* small palette knife
* baking tray
* greaseproof paper
* wire cooling rack

1 Place all the ingredients for the hot mix in a deep heavy saucepan and bring to the boil, stirring (see 1).

2 Remove the pan from the heat and, using a wooden spoon, carefully stir in the butter (see 2).

3 Once well combined, add the bicarbonate of soda and whisk the mixture through briefly.

4 Pour into the bowl of a Kitchen Aid or electric mixer and leave to cool until it is just slightly warm.

5 Once cooled, sieve the flour over the top and combine on low speed, using the paddle attachment, until it forms a dough (see 3).

6 Wrap the dough in cling film and chill for a couple of hours or overnight.

7 Place the dough on a floured clean surface and knead it briefly. Then roll it between two ¼ inch (5mm) guide sticks to an even thickness.

8 Use cookie cutters to cut out shapes and, using a palette knife, lay these on a baking tray lined with greaseproof paper.

9 Chill again for about 30 minutes. Preheat the oven to 200°C, gas 6.

10 Bake the cookies in the preheated oven for about 10–12 minutes until just firm to the touch.

11 Lift off the tray and allow to cool on a wire rack. Wrapped in foil or cling film, they will keep well in a cool dry place for up to a month (as will the basic sugar cookies opposite).

baking basic cakes ~~~~~~

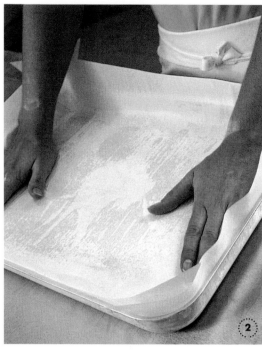

For the best-tasting basic sponge, you really need to ensure that you only use the best-quality ingredients – butter, flour, eggs and sugar, as well as flavourings – even if they are that bit more expensive. Personally, I am a big fan of organic products and free-range eggs.

BASIC VICTORIA SPONGE

MAKES ONE 12 X 16 INCH (30 X 40CM) BAKING TRAY OR TWO 8 INCH (20CM) BAKING TINS OR ABOUT 50 CUP CAKES

400g salted butter, softened
400g caster sugar
8 medium eggs, at room temperature
400g self-raising flour
a little vegetable oil

OPTIONAL FLAVOURS:

for vanilla sponge, add seeds from
   2 vanilla pods
for lemon sponge, add finely grated
   zest of 4 lemons
for orange sponge, add finely grated
   zest of 4 oranges
for chocolate sponge, replace 100g of
   the self-raising flour with 100g of
   cocoa powder and add 100g
   melted dark Belgian chocolate to
   the butter-and-sugar mix

EQUIPMENT

✳ Kitchen Aid or electric mixer with
   paddle attachment
✳ bowl
✳ baking tins, for large cakes
✳ baking tray, for fondant fancies
✳ muffin tray and paper cases, for
   cup cakes
✳ greaseproof paper
✳ large palette knife, small spoon or
✳ large paper piping bag (see page 25)
✳ wire cooling rack

inside it so it will go up the sides and be slightly higher than the sides all round (see 1), just in case the sponge rises higher than them. Snip into the four corners so it will sit neatly (see 2). Fill evenly with the mixture, using a large palette knife (see 4).

6 For cup cakes, place the paper cases in the muffin tray and fill with the cake mix only up to half of their height. You can either use a small spoon or pipe the mix into the paper cases with the help of a large paper piping bag.

7 Bake a large tray or tin for about 25 minutes, and cup cakes for only about 12–15 minutes. Test the sponge with a thin knife; it should come out clean when the sponge is cooked through.

8 Lift off the tray and allow to cool on a wire rack. Wrap in cling film to keep for up to a day in a cool dry place. If you need to keep for longer, then wrap and store in the fridge for up to a week, or freeze.

MY FAVOURITE CAKE AND FILLING COMBINATIONS

My cake recipes are very easy to make, but it is important that even the simplest cake is bursting with flavour. Below are some suggestions of my favourite combinations to guarantee this.

When flavouring sugar syrups and buttercreams, always do this the day before and let them infuse overnight, as the flavour will then develop even more strongly.

It is important that a sponge is well soaked with sugar syrup, as this gives it moisture and lots of flavour.

FOR VANILLA AND RASPBERRY CAKE USE:

✳ Vanilla sponge
✳ Vanilla sugar syrup (see page 15) for soaking
✳ Vanilla buttercream (see page 14) and raspberry jam for layering

FOR LEMON AND LIMONCELLO CAKE USE:

✳ Lemon sponge
✳ Sugar syrup (see page 15) flavoured with lemon zest and Limoncello liqueur for soaking
✳ Lemon curd (I use a good-quality ready-made) and lemon-flavoured buttercream (see page 14) for layering

FOR ORANGE AND GRAND MARNIER CAKE USE:

✳ Orange sponge
✳ Sugar syrup (see page 15) flavoured with orange zest and Grand Marnier for soaking
✳ Luxury orange marmalade (again from the supermarket) and orange-flavoured buttercream (see page 14) for layering

FOR CHOCOLATE AND PEPPERMINT CAKE USE:

✳ Chocolate sponge
✳ Sugar syrup (see page 15)
✳ Belgian chocolate ganache (see page 15) flavoured with peppermint liqueur for layering

1 Preheat the oven to 200°C, gas 6.

2 Place the butter, sugar and chosen flavouring in the bowl of an electric mixer and, using the paddle attachment, cream together until pale and fluffy.

3 Beat the eggs lightly in another bowl and slowly add to the mix, while paddling on medium speed. If the mixture starts curdling, add a little bit of flour.

4 Once the eggs and the butter mixture are combined, mix in the flour at low speed.

5 For fondant fancies or large cakes, grease a baking tray or tin with a little vegetable oil. Cut a piece of greaseproof paper to fit

basic cake fillings ~~~~~~~~~~~~~~~~~~~~~~~~~~~~~~~

The syrups and fillings I give here have proven to be among my most popular. You can, though, use anything you fancy that tastes good, and ring endless changes on these basic tastes.

BUTTERCREAM FROSTING

MAKES 500G

250g soft unsalted butter

250g icing sugar, sifted

OPTIONAL FLAVOURS:

seeds from a vanilla pod

finely grated lemon zest

finely grated orange zest

EQUIPMENT

✳ Kitchen Aid or electric mixer with
   paddle attachment

1 Place the butter, sugar and flavouring in the bowl of an electric mixer and, using a paddle attachment (see 1), beat on medium speed until light and fluffy (see 2).

2 If not using immediately, store in a sealed container in the fridge and bring back to room temperature before use.

SUGAR SYRUP

MAKES ABOUT 500ML

250ml sugar

OPTIONAL FLAVOURS:

seeds from a vanilla pod

finely grated lemon zest and
   Limoncello liqueur

finely grated orange zest and
   Grand Marnier liqueur

peppermint liqueur

EQUIPMENT

✳ saucepan

✳ spoon

1 Place the sugar and 250ml water
in a saucepan, stir well and bring
to the boil. Let it cool down.

2 When lukewarm, add the
flavourings. Store in the refrigerator
if not using immediately.

BELGIAN CHOCOLATE GANACHE

MAKES ABOUT 500G

250ml single cream

250g dark couverture chocolate
   drops (I use 55% cocoa – any
   darker and it splits more readily)

OPTIONAL FLAVOURS:

orange or peppermint liqueur, or any
   other liqueur

EQUIPMENT

✳ saucepan

✳ bowl

✳ whisk

1 Place the cream in a saucepan
and bring to the boil.

2 Place the chocolate in a bowl.
Pour the cream over (see 1) and
stir together using a whisk (see 2).

3 Let cool slightly, until just
beginning to harden (see 3),
before use.

4 If not using immediately,
store in a sealed container in the
fridge and bring back to room
temperature before use.

filling and covering large cakes ɛɛɛɛɛɛɛɛɛɛɛɛɛɛɛɛɛɛɛ

The following instructions for various standard procedures cover all aspects of filling and assembling large and tiered cakes. Although the cake used here is square, the basic techniques demonstrated work equally well with round cakes, or any other shape.

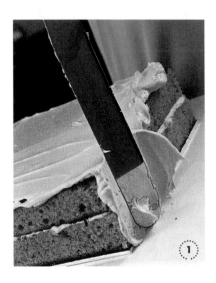

MAKING A SQUARE TWO-TIERED CAKE

10 INCH (25CM) AND 7 INCH (17.5CM)

You'll need exactly this procedure for making the Dropping Daisies cake on page 135, for example.

two 10 inch (25cm) square sponges
(1 recipe quantity of basic Victoria sponge, see page 12)

two 7 inch (17.5cm) square sponges
(½ recipe quantity of basic Victoria sponge, see page 12)

250ml sugar syrup (see page 15), flavoured to your choice

750g buttercream (see page 14), flavoured to your choice

plus a filling of your choice (e.g. lemon curd or orange marmalade)

EQUIPMENT

✳ bread knife
✳ 10 inch (25cm) and 7 inch (17.5cm) thin square cake boards
✳ pastry brush
✳ large palette knife
✳ side scraper
✳ 2 trays, large enough for the cakes and able to fit in your fridge

1 Using a bread knife, trim the top crust off the two larger sponges.

2 Place one of the sponges on a 10 inch (25cm) cake board with a dab of buttercream to make it stick.

3 Using a pastry brush, soak the top of this layer well with the sugar syrup and then spread it with a thin layer of buttercream.

4 Soak the second sponge with sugar syrup as well. Then spread this with the chosen filling.

5 Turn this sponge upside down and place it on the bottom layer so that the buttercream and filling come together.

6 Soak the top of the sandwiched cake with sugar syrup.

7 Place the entire cake on top of the turntable and coat the outside of the cake with buttercream (see 1), spreading it first over the top, then down along the sides.

8 Use the palette knife to level the top and a side scraper to straighten the sides (see 2).

9 Repeat the buttercream coating until you are happy with the shape. The cake should be level and straight for best results.

10 Repeat this entire process with the 7 inch (17.5cm) sponge. Chill both cakes for at least one hour, until the buttercream has set firmly.

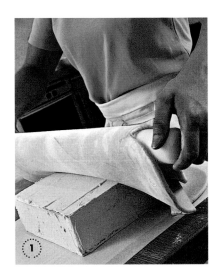

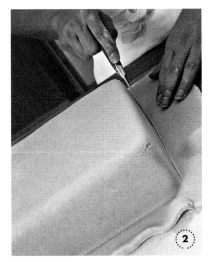

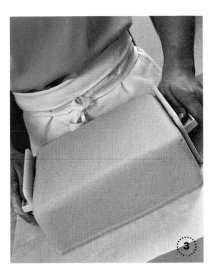

COVERING A CAKE WITH MARZIPAN AND SUGAR PASTE

icing sugar for dusting

2.5kg white marzipan

a little buttercream (see page 14)

2.5kg white sugar paste

food colour (here mint green)

alcohol or water, for brushing

EQUIPMENT

✳ large rolling pin

✳ ¼ inch (5mm) guide sticks

✳ greaseproof paper

✳ large palette knife

✳ small kitchen knife

✳ cake smoothers

✳ pastry brush

✳ paper piping bag (see page 25)

1 Start at least 2 days ahead. Place the cake on a sheet of greaseproof paper. Using a palette knife, apply a thin coat of buttercream all over to help the marzipan stick.

2 First work on the 10 inch (25cm) tier: dust a work surface with icing sugar, put 1.5kg marzipan on it and, with a rolling pin and ¼ inch (5mm) guide sticks, roll to an even thickness large enough to cover the tier.

3 Using the rolling pin, lift the marzipan and lay it over the cake (see 1). Push it down the sides with your hand and ensure there are no air pockets.

4 Trim excess marzipan off the sides with a kitchen knife (see 2).

5 Run the cake smoother along the sides and over the top of the cake until they all look nice and straight (see 3).

6 Repeat this complete process for the 7 inch (17.5cm) tier, using the remaining marzipan.

7 Let the marzipan set for 1 to 2 days at a cool room temperature.

8 When the marzipan is firmly set, knead all the sugar paste with some suitable food colour until it has an even hue.

9 Brush a thin layer of alcohol or water over the larger marzipan-covered cake.

10 On a surface dusted with icing sugar, roll out 1.5 kg of the sugar paste between ¼ inch (5mm) guide sticks. Use to cover the cake following the same procedure as for applying the marzipan.

11 Repeat this process for the smaller cake, using the remaining sugar paste. Let the sugar paste set for 1 or 2 days at room temperature.

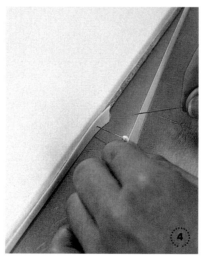

1 Dust the cake board thinly with icing sugar and brush it with a little water (this will make a glue for the sugar paste).

2 Roll the sugar paste out to about ⅛ inch (3 mm) thick and large enough to cover the cake board.

3 Use the rolling pin, lift the paste and lay it over the cake board (see 1).

4 Let the cake smoother glide carefully over the surface of the paste and push out any trapped air bubbles.

5 Place the board on top of the turntable, if using one, and push the paste down the sides with the cake smoother (see 2).

6 Trim the excess paste off with a palette knife (see 3) and let the sugar paste dry for 1 or 2 days.

7 Once the paste is dry, wind the ribbon around the edge of the board and fix the ends with a metal pin (see 4).

COVERING A CAKE BOARD WITH SUGAR PASTE

icing sugar for dusting
250g coloured sugar paste

EQUIPMENT
* 14 inch (35cm) square cake board
* pastry brush
* rolling pin
* cake smoothers
* turntable (optional)
* palette knife
* 1.45m white satin ribbon, 15mm wide
* metal pin

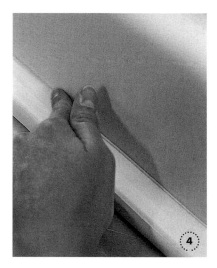

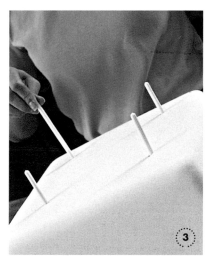

TIERED CAKES

150g soft-peak royal icing (see page 24)

food colour of choice (here mint green)

EQUIPMENT

* 14 inch (35cm) iced cake board (see opposite)
* paper piping bags (see page 25)
* large step palette knife
* 5 inch (12.5cm) square template
* small needle
* 4 plastic dowels
* pencil
* strong scissors or serrated knife

1 Pipe some icing in the centre of the board to help secure the cake. Using the step palette knife, lift the larger tier (pages 16–17) and place in the centre of the board (see 1).

2 Place a 5 inch (12.5cm) square template in the centre of the top of the lower tier and mark each corner with a needle (see 2).

3 Push a plastic dowel down into the cake at each mark (see 3). These will stop the top tier sinking into the bottom. Mark with a pencil where it comes out of the cake.

4 Lift out the dowels and, using strong scissors or a serrated knife, trim them 1mm above the mark, then stick them back into the cake

5 Pipe some royal icing into the middle of the bottom tier to secure the top tier in place and centre the top tier on the bottom one.

6 Mix some icing with food colour to match the sugar paste and pipe a thin line along the bottom edge of each tier. While wet, run a finger over them to smooth (see 4).

Made from sugar, water and cream of tartar, fondant is widely used in confectionery as well as in cake-decorating. To keep it simple, I use ready-made fondant, which is available from specialist suppliers or (in a powdered version) from supermarkets. Tightly wrapped in cling film, it will keep for up to 3 months. It is important not to allow the fondant to boil at any time.

FONDANT ICING

MAKES ENOUGH FOR ABOUT 30 CUP CAKES OR 50 FONDANT FANCIES

1.5kg ready-made fondant (see above)

150ml sugar syrup (see page 15)

1 tablespoon lemon juice

1 tablespoon liquid glucose

selection of food colours

EQUIPMENT

* large microwave-proof bowl

* microwave cooker

* large wooden or plastic spoon

1 Place the fondant in a large microwave-proof bowl, cover with hot water and leave it to soften for about 15 minutes.

2 Pour away the water and add the remaining ingredients.

4 tablespoons sugar syrup (see
   page 15), flavoured as you prefer

FOR 12 FONDANT ICED CUP CAKES:

100g sieved apricot jam

400g fondant icing and food colour of
   choice

FOR 12 CHOCOLATE CUP CAKES:

400g Belgian Chocolate Ganache (see
   page 15)

FOR 12 BUTTERCREAM CUP CAKES:

300g buttercream (see page 14)

EQUIPMENT

* pastry brush

* saucepan

* small bowl

* small palette knife or spoon

1 Using a pastry brush, soak the
top of each of the cup cakes with
sugar syrup.

2 For fondant iced cup cakes, boil
the sieved apricot jam with a little
water in a pan and brush it over
each cup cake. Let them dry.

3 Have your fondant icing ready in
a small bowl and dip the top of each
cup cake into the icing (see above).

4 Let the icing set and repeat
the dipping process again for an
even coating.

5 For chocolate or buttercream
cup cakes, simply spread the
topping over each cake using a
small palette knife or spoon.

3 Heat in the microwave cooker
for about 3 minutes at medium
power. Stir to combine well, then
heat for another minute.

4 For dipping cup cakes and
fondant fancies, divide the fondant
among small bowls and colour each
with different food colours, adding
them a little drop at a time.

5 Before you start dipping, heat
one of the bowls in the microwave
for about 10–20 seconds at full heat.

You want the fondant to be very
warm (not boiling) to the touch.

6 Check the consistency of the
fondant. If it feels thick and heavy
when dipping, add a little more
sugar syrup to thin it down until
it runs smoothly.

CUP CAKES

FOR 12 CUP CAKES:

12 cup cakes (see Basic Victoria
   Sponge, page 12)

FONDANT FANCIES

Using the fondant icing as shown on the previous pages, we can now make basic little fondant fancies. During my time working for Konditor & Cook, I must have produced literally thousands of such little fondant cakes – an experience that undoubtedly influenced my style. I now like to use lots of glitter and lustre on them, as you can see in my fondant Heart Fancies on pages 70–71 and my signature Bollywood Kitsch Cakes on pages 66–7, etc.

FOR ABOUT 35

1 rectangular tray of
   vanilla sponge (see page 12)
150ml vanilla-flavoured
   sugar syrup (see page 14)
150g vanilla buttercream
   (see page 14)
150g seedless raspberry jam

1kg fondant icing (see page 20-21)
selection of food colours
200g sieved apricot jam
100g icing sugar
500g marzipan

EQUIPMENT

 ✳ bread knife
 ✳ tray
 ✳ cling film
 ✳ small bowls
 ✳ pastry brush
 ✳ large rolling pin
 ✳ heart-shaped cutter, if required
 ✳ microwave cooker
 ✳ truffle fork
 ✳ wire cooling rack
 ✳ muffin paper cases

1 Using the bread knife, trim off the dark top layer from your sponge and then turn it upside down on a tray.

2 Cut the sponge horizontally in half. Set the top half aside.

3 Using a pastry brush, soak the top surface of the bottom sponge with the vanilla syrup and spread it with the buttercream and then the raspberry jam. Sandwich with the top half of the sponge. Wrap in cling film and chill for at least 2 hours.

4 While it is chilling, prepare the fondant icing: divide in among small bowls and mix with different food colours of your choice. Cover each bowl with cling film and set aside.

5 Once the sponge is cool and firm, warm up the apricot jam, unwrap the sponge and, using the pastry brush, spread a thin layer of jam over the top.

6 Dust your working surface with icing sugar and roll the marzipan out on it to a thickness of 3mm. Cut it to the same size as the sponge, lift it with your rolling pin and lay it on top of the sponge (see 1).

7 Slice the marzipan-topped sponge into 5cm squares (see 2), or use the cutter to cut out heart shapes.

8 Brush the top of each piece with more apricot glaze.

9 Reheat a bowlful of coloured fondant gently in the microwave on medium for 20 seconds at a time, until it is warm and runny (alternatively, heat it in a heavy pan over very low heat, stirring constantly, if you don't have a microwave). Do not allow the fondant to boil, or it will lose its shine.

10 Give the fondant a quick stir and start dipping your little cakes in it. First dip the cake into the fondant upside-down. To lift it out, hold it with one finger at the bottom of the cake and with a truffle fork at the top (see 3). Make sure you don't push the fork into the marzipan, just lift the cake gently and place it straight on to the wire cooling rack (see 4), then leave it for the icing to set.

11 Carefully remove the cakes from the rack and place in paper cases. This is best done with slightly wet fingers, to prevent the icing sticking to them.

STIFF-PEAK CONSISTENCY

SOFT-PEAK CONSISTENCY

RUNNY CONSISTENCY

Making and using royal icing is perhaps the most essential skill in cake decorating, but a lot easier than you might think. If you do find it daunting, you can always buy a ready-to-mix version from a supermarket. This recipe may make a lot, but these quantities are easier to mix.

ROYAL ICING

MAKES ABOUT 1.2KG

25g merriwhite (dried egg white powder)

1kg icing sugar, sifted

1 tablespoon lemon juice

EQUIPMENT

* sieve
* Kitchen Aid or electric mixer with paddle attachment
* spoon
* sealable plastic container
* j-cloth

1 Mix the merriwhite with 150ml water and pass through a sieve to get rid of any lumps.

2 Place the icing sugar in the clean bowl of an electric mixer, add about three-quarters of the merriwhite mixture and the lemon juice, and start mixing on low speed.

3 Once the sugar and the merriwhite are well combined, check the consistency. If the sides of the bowl still look dry and crumbly, add some more merriwhite until the icing looks almost smooth but not wet.

4 Keep mixing for about 4–5 minutes, until it has reached stiff-peak consistency.

5 Spoon into a plastic container, cover with a clean damp j-cloth and the lid. Store at room temperature.

ROYAL ICING CONSISTENCIES

Throughout the book, I will refer to three useful consistencies of royal icing, which are important in achieving the right results. Simply thin down your basic royal icing with water, a little bit at a time, mixing with a palette knife, until you have the right consistency. Keep your icing covered with cling film or a damp cloth when not using it, to stop it from drying out.

STIFF-PEAK CONSISTENCY

for piping sugar flowers and leaves

SOFT-PEAK CONSISTENCY

for piping lines, dots and borders

RUNNY CONSISTENCY

for filling in the centres of spaces

MAKING A PIPING BAG

1 Take a square of greaseproof paper about 14 x 14 inches (35 x 35cm) and fold a corner over to the opposite corner. Cut through the fold with a sharp knife (see 1).

2 Take one of the resulting paper triangles and hold it with your left hand at the middle of the longest side and with your right hand at the corner on the opposite (see 2). Move your right hand over to the right corner and curl it over to the top corner, so it forms a cone (see 3).

3 Now move your left hand to the left corner and roll it around the cone until all corners meet at the top back of the cone. Adjust by moving them back and forth between your thumb and fingers until the cone forms a sharp point (see 4).

4 Now fold the corners over to the inside of the cone, tear it at each side of the seam and fold the flap inside. This ensures the cone will stay in shape without opening up (see 5).

5 To fill the bag, hold it in one hand and use a small palette knife to fill it with the icing using the other hand. Don't fill it more than half full, or the icing will squeeze out through the top when piping.

6 Close by folding the side with the seam over to the plain side twice.

BASIC PIPING TECHNIQUES

First snip a small tip off your piping bag already filled with icing.

PIPING LINES:

1 Hold the bag between thumb and fingers of your preferred hand and use the index finger of your other hand to guide the nozzle.

2 Touch the starting point with the tip of the bag and slowly squeeze out icing. As you squeeze, lift the bag slightly and pull the line straight towards you or, say, along the sides of a cookie.

3 As you approach the finishing point, gradually bring the bag down, stop squeezing and drop the line by touching the finishing point.

PIPING DOTS:

1 Holding tip 1mm above surface, squeeze icing to produce a dot. Gradually lift tip as dot gets larger.

2 Once the dot is its desired size, stop squeezing and lift off the tip.

3 Should the dot form a little peak at the top, flatten it carefully with a damp soft artist's brush.

PIPING DOTTED BORDERS:

1 Start as for piping a dot. Once the dot has reached the required size, stop squeezing and pull the tip of your bag down, stopping where the next dot should start.

2 Repeat, making sure the dots are all the same size and equidistant. After a short while, you will get into a flowing motion and your border will look nice and even.

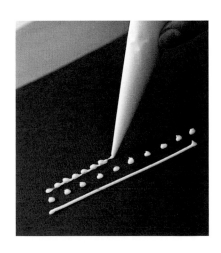

DAFFODILS

SIMPLE 5-PETAL

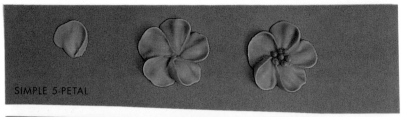

PANSIES

DAISIES

ROYAL ICED FLOWERS

Remember that for the piping of almost all flower shapes, you will want to use icing with a stiff-peak consistency.

EQUIPMENT

* metal piping nozzles for petal piping (e.g. Wilton 104, PME 56R, 57R, 58R)
* greaseproof paper
* scissors
* flower nail
* paper piping bags (see page 25)

food colours of choice

edible ink pen (black)

PIPING SIMPLE 5-PETAL FLOWERS:

1 From a sheet of greaseproof paper, cut small squares slightly larger than the flower to be piped.

2 Make a paper piping bag and snip the tip off the empty bag to produce an opening large enough to fit a metal piping tube. Drop a Wilton 104 or PME 58R piping nozzle inside the bag, narrow end first.

3 Fill the bag with appropriately coloured stiff-peak icing.

4 Pipe a small dot of icing on top of the flower nail, stick one of the paper squares on top and hold the nail in one hand.

5 Hold the piping bag in the other hand at a 45 degree angle to the nail, with the wide end touching the centre of the flower nail and the narrow end pointing out and slightly raised.

6 Squeeze out the first petal and give the nail a one-fifth turn as you move the nozzle out towards the edge of the flower nail. Use less pressure as you are moving back towards the centre and curve the nozzle slightly to give the petal a natural shape. Stop squeezing as the wide end touches the centre of the nail and lift up the nozzle.

7 Repeat this 4 more times to make all the petals.

8 Remove the flower with its base paper from the nail and leave it to dry.

9 Pipe small yellow dots into the centres as stamens.

Note: for smaller flowers, simply use one of the smaller piping tubes listed.

PIPING DAISIES:

1 Use a Wilton 104 piping tube and some stiff-peak white royal icing.

2 Prepare your piping bag and paper squares for the flower nail as above.

3 Mark the centre of the paper-lined nail with a dot of icing.

4 Start at the outer edge of the nail, holding the wide end away from the centre and the narrow end towards the centre of nail.

5 Slightly touch the paper with the wide end of the piping nozzle, squeeze out the icing and pull the nozzle towards the middle as you release the pressure. Stop and pull the tip away.

6 Repeat for 8 or more petals, while turning the nail appropriately (**see** below).

7 Remove the flower with the base paper from the nail and leave to dry.

8 Pipe small yellow dots into the centres as stamens.

Note: for smaller flowers, simply use one of the smaller piping tubes.

PIPING PANSIES:

1 You will need 2 piping bags with 2 piping tubes of the same size, one filled with yellow and one filled with purple stiff-peak icing.

2 Start with the yellow icing. Pipe 2 petals next to each other following the same piping technique as for the simple 5-petal flower above.

3 Repeat and pipe 2 shorter yellow petals on top of the larger ones.

4 For the large base petal, tuck the nozzle with the purple icing under the right side of the large yellow petal and start squeezing out a petal the same width as the larger petals, using a back-and-forth hand motion for a ruffled effect.

5 Remove the flower with the paper from the nail and leave to dry.

6 Using a pen filled with edible black ink, draw fine lines into the centre of the pansy.

7 Pipe a fine yellow loop in the middle as a stamen.

PIPING DAFFODILS:

1 Using a PME 58R piping nozzle and egg-yellow stiff-peak icing, pipe a 6-petal flower on top of a paper-lined flower nail, using the same technique as for the daisy.

2 Remove the flower with the base paper from the nail and leave to dry.

3 Pipe 3 rings of pale orange icing on top of each other into the centre of the flower and let the icing dry.

4 Once dry, pipe a fine ruffled line over the edge of the circle.

marzipan roses ~~~~~~

I am a big fan of marzipan or sugar roses, but I do have to say that it took me a while to master the perfect rose. You might also need a little time until you are happy with your results, but let me tell you now that in most cases it is actually the sheer quantity of the roses that makes the cake.

FOR ABOUT 6 LARGE OR 12 SMALL ROSES OR 20 ROSEBUDS:

250g neutral marzipan (you can use
    sugar paste instead)
pink food colour
green food colour

EQUIPMENT

* 2 sheets of cellophane
* small rolling pin
* rose calyx cutter
* rose leaf cutter
* leaf veiner

Colour 100g of the marzipan pale pink, 100g dark pink and 50g green.

TO MAKE ROSEBUDS:

1 You will need 2 hazelnut-sized balls of dark pink marzipan and one twice as large.

2 Place these pieces of marzipan between 2 sheets of cellophane (see 1) and, starting with the larger one, push it down sideways to make it longer, and then flatten one long side with your thumb until very thin (see 2).

3 For the other petals, push a smaller ball down with your thumb, starting from the centre to one side, until it forms a round petal with one thick and one thin side. Repeat with the other.

4 Roll the large petal to a spiral shape, thin side up (see 3). This will form the centre of the rose.

5 Take one of the smaller petals, thin side up, and lay it around the centre over the seam (see 4).

6 Tuck the third petal slightly inside the second and squeeze it around the centre (see 5).

7 Slightly curve the petal edges out with your fingertips (see 6).

TO MAKE SMALL ROSES:

8 Continue by laying another 3 petals of the same size around the rosebud, each slightly overlapping.

9 Again, slightly curve the edge of the petals out with your fingertips.

TO MAKE LARGE ROSES:

10 Continue by laying another 5 petals of the same size around the rosebud, each slightly overlapping.

11 Slightly curve the edge of the petals out with your fingertips. To finish, pinch excess marzipan off the bottom.

TO MAKE CALYCES AND LEAVES:

12 Roll out some green marzipan between the 2 sheets of cellophane.

13 Cut a calyx out with the rose calyx cutter and stick it underneath the bottom of the rose (marzipan will stick to itself; for sugar paste use a little bit of water).

14 Pinch and shape the tips with your fingers as required.

15 Cut the leaves out with the rose leaf cutter.

16 Press in the rose leaf veiner (see 8) and shape slightly with your fingers for a natural look (see 9).

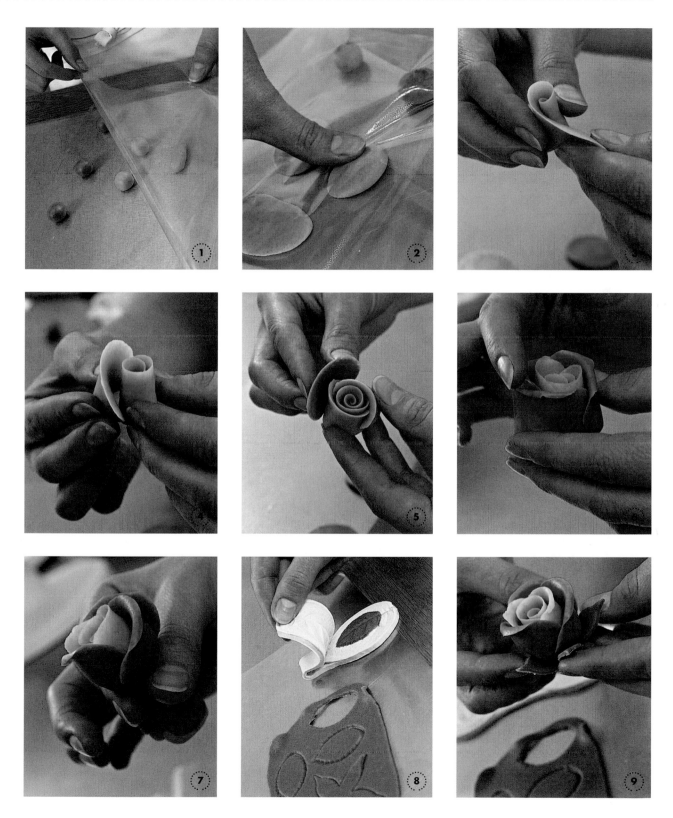

cookies

alphabet cookies

Alphabet cookies are very easy to make, even for beginners, as only the most basic of piping techniques are required. You can use the finished cookies to lay out names on your party table or arrange them into little messages (such as 'HAPPY BIRTHDAY', 'I LOVE YOU', 'THANK YOU', 'CONGRATULATIONS') and wrap them in beautiful gift boxes.

FOR ABOUT 10-12 COOKIES
selection of food colours
about 300 g royal icing (see page 24)
selection of 10–12 chocolate cookies
 (see page 10), made in letter shapes
 of your choice

EQUIPMENT
* bowls
* small palette knife for mixing
* paper piping bags (see page 25)

1 Choose your colours and prepare one piping bag with soft-peak icing and another bag of runny icing in each colour.

2 Using soft-peak icing, first pipe the outline of each cookie.

3 When you have finished, take the bag of runny icing in the same colour and fill in the centres.

4 Leave the cookies to dry for about 1 hour before use.

PEGGY

bollywood heart lollies

It is simplicity itself to turn a simple shaped cookie into an attractive and fun lolly by embedding a lolly stick into the mixture before baking, as below. Decorated dramatically – here I've gone for Bollywood glamour, like the cup cakes on pages 66–7 – they make the most charming of gifts.

FOR 6 COOKIE LOLLIES

food colours (yellow, orange, pink,
    blue and purple)

300g royal icing (see page 24)

6 heart-shaped gingerbread cookies
    (see page 11) baked on a lolly stick
    (see 1 and 2 above)

gold glitter

50g pastel-pink sugar paste

pink shimmer

EQUIPMENT

✳ bowls

✳ small palette knife

✳ paper piping bags (see page 25)

✳ small piece of greaseproof paper

✳ thin soft artist's brush

✳ push-in rose mould

✳ thick soft artist's brush

✳ six 50cm lengths of organza ribbon
    in different colours (50cm per lolly)

1 First mix your colours and prepare your piping bags. You will need 1 bag of white soft-peak icing and 1 each of runny icing in bright yellow, orange, pink, blue, green (yellow + blue) and purple.

2 Using the white soft-peak icing, pipe the outline of the heart, then pipe dots evenly spaced around the outline (see 3).

3 Drizzle a layer of gold glitter on a piece of greaseproof paper and dip each cookie into the glitter while the outline icing is still wet. You want the outline and the dots completely covered with glitter. Let dry.

4 Remove the excess glitter with a thin soft artist's brush (see 4).

5 Fill in the centre of each heart with a different colour of runny icing and let dry.

6 Shape a small piece of sugar paste into a ball and push it into the rose mould (see 5). Remove it from the mould by bending the mould until the paste comes out automatically. Repeat to make 5 more in the same way.

7 Using a thick soft artist's brush, dust the roses with the edible shimmer (see 6).

8 Stick one rose into the centre of each heart with a small dot of icing.

9 Fill a piping bag with pastel-green soft-peak icing and snip off the tip in a 'V' shape. Use to pipe small leaves around the roses. Let dry.

10 Tie a piece of ribbon around the top of the lolly stick.

flower basket cookies

A friend of mine once asked me for a gift idea for the flower girls at her wedding, so I came up with these flower basket cookies in the colours of the wedding flowers. Delicately wrapped in tissue paper and presented in a lovely gift box as shown overleaf, they also make a perfect little gift for Mother's Day or even just a little token to say 'thank you' to someone.

FOR 6 BASKET COOKIES AND 12 MINI FLOWER COOKIES

6 vanilla cookies (see page 10) in the
    shape of a basket

12 vanilla circular cookies (see page 10),
    about 1½ inch (3.75cm) in diameter

12 mini sugar blossoms in each of
    three colours: pink, purple and
    white (see pages 26–7)

500g Royal Icing (see page 24)

food colours (yellow, pink, purple)

EQUIPMENT

✳ bowls

✳ small palette knife

✳ paper piping bags (see page 25)

✳ Wilton piping nozzle 103

TO MAKE THE BASKETS:

1 First mix your colours and prepare your icing bags. You will need 2 piping bags filled with soft-peak icing, one in pastel pink and the other in pastel purple, together with 2 piping bags filled with runny icing in the same colours.

2 Using pink and purple soft-peak icing, pipe the outline of 3 baskets, including the handle, in each colour.

3 Fill in the centre of each cookie with runny icing of the same colour as the outline. Let dry.

4 Stick 6 sugar blossoms (2 of each colour) into the centre of each basket and let them cascade down.

5 Finish the look by piping little green leaves next to the flowers as shown opposite .

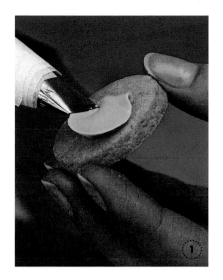

TO MAKE THE MINI FLOWER COOKIES:

To make a selection of pink, purple and white flower cookies, follow the same technique as in Royal Iced Flowers on pages 26–7. Use the cookie as you would use the flower nail (without the paper, of course) and pipe the flower directly on it, using nozzle 103 (see 1–3). Once these are dry, snip a 'v'-shape from the tip of a paper piping bag (see 4) and use it to pipe little green leaves around the flowers (see 5).

'a perfect little gift for Mother's Day'

underwater world

Loving everything about the ocean as I do, I was ecstatic when I came across this gorgeous set of waterworld cookie cutters. I couldn't wait to design bright multicoloured tropical fish, sea horses and seashells. For this more grown-up version, I have kept the colours more subtle. The lobster, for example, would work well as a place card at a seafood-themed dinner party.

If you are making a selection of these cookies, first prepare all your colours and piping bags. Then pipe all the cookie outlines first, so that when you have finished with the last cookie, you can start filling in the centre of the first cookie. Continue in this way and you will save yourself a lot of time waiting for icing to dry.

FOR 6 COOKIES
food colours (red, orange, brown,
    violet, dusky pink, blue, moss green
    and yellow)
300g royal icing (see page 24)
6 gingerbread cookies (see page 11) in
    the shapes of a lobster, a tropical
    fish, a starfish, a sea horse, a
    seashell and an octopus

EQUIPMENT
* bowl
* small palette knife
* paper piping bags (see page 25)

TO MAKE THE LOBSTER:

1 First prepare your colours and piping bags. To make the red used, mix your icing with red food colour and a little bit of brown food colour. You will need 1 bag of this in soft-peak icing. To make the orange used, mix your icing with orange food colour and a little bit of red food colour. You will need 1 bag of this in soft-peak and another in runny icing.

2 Using the soft-peak orange icing, pipe the outline of the lobster.

3 Using the runny orange icing, fill in the centres. Let dry.

4 Repeat the piping of the outlines, but this time using red icing. Also divide the body parts and give the lobster eyes and add some detail to the tail. Let dry.

TO MAKE THE TROPICAL FISH:

1 First prepare your colours and piping bags. To make the green, mix your icing with moss-green food colour and a little bit of yellow food colour. You will need one bag of this in soft-peak icing and another in runny icing. You will also need one bag with yellow runny icing.

2 Using the green soft-peak icing, pipe the outlines, including the stripes of the fish.

3 Using green runny icing, fill in the face, the middle part of the fish and the tail. Let dry.

4 Using the yellow runny icing, fill in the remaining parts. Let dry.

5 Using the green soft-peak icing, repeat the piping of the outlines again, and add some detail to the fins.

6 Also pipe the eye using the yellow icing. Let dry.

TO MAKE THE STARFISH:

1 First prepare your colours and piping bags. To make the yellow, mix your icing with yellow food colour and a little bit of brown food colour. You will need one bag of this in soft-peak icing and another in runny icing. To make the orange, mix your icing with orange food colour and a little bit of brown food colour. You will need one bag of this in soft-peak icing.

2 Using the yellow soft-peak icing, pipe the outline of the starfish.

3 Using the yellow runny icing, fill in the centre. Let dry.

4 Repeat the piping of the outline, but this time using the orange icing, and pipe some dots into the centre of the starfish. Let dry.

TO MAKE THE SEA HORSE:

1 First mix your colours. To make the blue, mix your icing with blue food colour and a little bit of violet food colour. You will need 1 bag of this in soft-peak icing and another in runny icing. To make the green, mix your icing with moss-green food colour and yellow food colour. You will need 1 bag of this in soft-peak icing.

2 Using the blue soft-peak icing, pipe the outline of the sea horse.

3 Using the runny blue icing, fill in the centre. Let dry.

4 Using the green soft-peak icing, pipe the outline of the sea horse and give some detail to the body parts. Let dry.

TO MAKE THE SEASHELL:

1 First prepare your colours and piping bags. To make the pink, mix your icing with dusky-pink food colour. You will need 1 bag of this in soft-peak icing and another in runny icing. To make the purple, mix your icing with violet food colour and a little bit of dusky-pink food colour. You will need 1 bag of this in runny icing.

2 Using the pink soft-peak icing, pipe the outline of the seashell. Also pipe a separation line for the purple front part of the shell.

3 Using the runny pink icing, fill in the main part of the shell. Let dry.

4 Using the runny purple icing, fill in the small front part of the shell. Let dry.

5 Using the soft-peak pink icing, pipe the outline and the individual sections again. Let dry.

TO MAKE THE OCTOPUS:

1 First prepare your colours and piping bags. To make the pink, mix your icing with dusky-pink food colour and a bit of violet food colour. You will need one bag of this in soft-peak icing. To make the purple, mix your icing with violet food colour. You will need one bag of this in soft-peak and another in runny icing.

2 Using the purple soft-peak icing, pipe the outline of the octopus.

3 Using the purple runny icing, fill in the centre. Let dry.

4 Using the pink soft-peak icing, pipe the outline again, and dots for the tentacles. Let dry.

Easter egg cookies

When I was a child, I used to love painting Easter eggs with my mum each year. Making these cookies is also child's play and a perfect thing to do if you are a beginner to decorating cookies. For an easy Easter gift you can even arrange a selection of eggs in various sizes with different designs in a suitably pretty basket and tie it with ribbon. See my Kaleidoscope Cakes on pages 64–5 for some more design ideas that might work well on egg-shaped cookies.

FOR 5 SMALL AND 5 LARGE COOKIES

5 small and 5 large lemon cookies
    (see page 10) in egg shapes
300g royal icing (see page 24)
selection of food colours

EQUIPMENT

✳ bowls
✳ small palette knife
✳ paper piping bags (see page 25)

1 Choose your background colours for your Easter egg cookies and prepare one bag of soft-peak and one bag of runny icing in each colour.

2 First pipe all the outlines, using the soft-peak icing.

3 Then fill the centres with the runny icing, using the same colour as for the outlines. Let set for about 1 hour.

4 Choose your colours for the decoration and start decorating the eggs with stripes and wavy lines using soft-peak icing; for dots, use thinned-down soft-peak icing.

birthday razzle dazzle

Decorating cookies is one of my favourite things to do as it is actually a lot easier than it looks. Create your own style, but keep your cookies smart and simple. Colourful patterns of dots and stripes piped on a plain background make very effective designs. You can either use them as a treat for guests at your own party – for instance, they make excellent place cards with guests' names written on them – or take them as gifts to a birthday party, presented stylishly gift-wrapped.

FOR ABOUT 10-12 COOKIES

selection of 10–12 cookies (see page 10)
**shaped like gift boxes and
birthday cakes**
about 400g royal icing (see page 24)
selection of food colours

EQUIPMENT

* **small palette knife**
* **paper piping bags** (see page 25)

FOR THE GIFT BOXES

1 First spread on the background colour: fill 1 piping bag with soft-peak royal icing and 1 with runny.

2 Using soft-peak icing, pipe the outline of the box and let set briefly. Then, with a bag of runny icing, fill in the centre of the box. Leave to dry for at least half an hour. Repeat with the remaining cookies and icing.

3 Choose a colour for the bow and fill one piping bag with soft-peak and one with runny icing in that colour. Pipe the outline and, once that sets, fill in the centre. Let dry.

4 Once the icing is completely dry, pipe the outline and the lines marking the individual sections once more to create a 3-D look.

FOR THE BIRTHDAY CAKES

5 Again, start with a background colour (white this time). Pipe the outline using soft-peak icing. Once set, fill in the centre with runny icing and let dry. Pipe the outline and the lines marking 'tiers' again.

6 Choose colours and decoration and prepare piping bags. For stripes, use soft-peak icing; for dots, thin down soft-peak icing with a little water to make it slightly runny.

7 Decorate the 'sides' with stripes or dots. Pipe a few candles on the 'top' with yellow icing for flames.

baby shower

What a quite perfect – and very personal gift – these will make for your best friend's baby shower. Wrap your selection of cute baby-themed cookies in an attractive presentation tin or box lined with tissue paper and tie it with a beautiful matching satin ribbon. If you already know the baby's name, why not pipe it on top of one of the cookies? If you don't know whether the baby is a girl or a boy, just make a mix of pink, blue and yellow iced cookies.

FOR 8 COOKIES

8 vanilla cookies (see page 10) in the shapes of a building block, a baby's bib, a pram, a baby's bottle, a baby sleep suit, 2 bootees and a rattle,

300g royal icing (see page 24)

food colours (pink, baby blue, yellow)

EQUIPMENT

* bowls
* small palette knife
* paper piping bags (see page 25)

First prepare your colours and piping bags. You will need 1 bag of soft-peak icing in each colour, 2 piping bags of runny white, 1 of runny blue icing and 1 small bag of runny yellow icing.

TO MAKE THE BUILDING BLOCK:

1 Using white soft-peak icing, pipe a white outline.

2 Using runny white icing, fill in the centre and let dry.

3 Using the blue soft-peak icing, pipe the outline again and the sides of the block, as well as the outlines for the alphabet letters.

4 Using runny blue icing, fill in the centres of the alphabet letters and let dry.

TO MAKE THE BABY'S BIB:

1 Using blue soft-peak icing, pipe the outline for the bow.

2 Using white soft-peak icing, pipe the outline for the bib.

3 Using blue runny icing, fill in the centre of the bow. Let dry.

4 Using white runny icing, fill in the centre of the bib. Let dry.

5 Using blue soft-peak icing, pipe the lines of the bow.

6 Using white soft-peak icing, pipe the outline of the bib again. Let dry.

'mixed pink, blue and yellow suits girls and boys'

TO MAKE THE PRAM:

1 Using white soft-peak icing, pipe the outline of the hood.

2 Using blue soft-peak icing, pipe the outline of the rest of the pram.

3 Using white runny icing, fill in the centre of the hood.

4 Using blue runny icing, pipe the outline of the rest of the pram. Let dry.

5 Using white soft-peak icing, pipe the outlines again, and the wheels, as well as adding some detail to the pram hood. Let dry.

TO MAKE THE BABY'S BOTTLE:

1 Using white soft-peak icing, pipe the outline for the bottle.

2 Using blue soft-peak icing, pipe the outline for the top in blue.

3 Using yellow soft-peak icing, pipe the outline for the dummy. Let dry.

4 Fill in the centres with runny icing using the same colours. Let dry.

5 Pipe the outlines of the individual parts again using the same icing as before.

6 Using white soft-peak icing, pipe a millilitre scale on the front of the bottle. Let dry.

TO MAKE THE BABY SLEEP SUIT:
Follow the same procedure as for the bootees (above right), piping the outline first, then fill in the centre and pipe the dots. Finish by repeating the outline and piping some details of the suit.

TO MAKE THE BOOTEES

1 Using white soft-peak icing, pipe the outlines for the bootees.

2 Using white runny icing, fill in the centres.

3 While that is still wet, use blue runny icing to pipe small dots all over the bootees, so that they level out with the white icing. Let everything dry.

4 Using blue soft-peak icing, pipe the blue ribbon bow.

6 Using white soft-peak icing, pipe the outline of the bootees again. Let dry.

TO MAKE THE RATTLE:
Follow the same procedure as for the bootees, piping the outline first, then fill in the centres and pipe the dots for the bow. Finish by repeating the outlines and details of the bow.

butterfly cookies

The challenge is to find the butterflies... this is just one of many examples of how an attractive piece of printed fabric can instantly inspire you into creating something simply gorgeous, like these brilliant little butterflies. Use these for a summer tea party or picnic lunch.

FOR ABOUT 10 COOKIES:

choice of food colour (here pastel pink)

300g royal icing (see page 24)

10 vanilla cookies in butterfly shape

 (see page 10)

EQUIPMENT

✳ bowls

✳ small palette knife

✳ paper piping bags (see page 25)

1 Prepare 1 piping bag of white soft-peak icing for the outline and the body, and one piping bag of runny pastel-pink icing for filling in the centre. For piping the little dots, thin down bright pink soft-peak icing with a little bit of water to make it slightly runny and put in a third bag.

2 Start by piping the white outline of the wings.

3 Once the outlines are set, fill in the wing centres with the pastel-pink icing. Let these dry for about half an hour.

4 Once the wings have dried, snip the tip of the piping bag containing the white icing to make it slightly larger and pipe the body between the wings, starting from the top and pulling it down towards you.

5 Finally, pipe little dots all over the wings, using your bright pink runny icing.

cookie catwalk

As if they have just come from the latest fashion shows in Paris or Milan, you can create your own cookie catwalk to reflect the season's latest trends and colours, using nothing more than the tip of a piping bag and some appropriately coloured icing.

FOR 12 COOKIES

12 chocolate cookies (see page 10)
   in the shape of handbags, dresses
   and shoes
500g royal icing (see page 24)
food colours (chocolate-brown, pink)

EQUIPMENT

✳ bowl
✳ small palette knife
✳ paper piping bags (see page 25)

First prepare your colours and piping bags. You will need 1 bag of soft-peak icing in each colour and 3–4 piping bags of runny icing in each colour.

TO MAKE THE HANDBAGS:

1 Using soft-peak icing in your colour of choice, pipe the outline of the body of the handbag.

2 Fill in the centre with runny icing of the same colour as for the outline. Let dry.

3 Using soft-peak icing of a different colour, repeat the piping of the outline and add details like a bow and the handbag handle. Let dry.

TO MAKE THE SHOES:

1 Using soft-peak icing in your colour of choice, pipe the outline of the shoe.

2 Fill in the centre with runny icing of the same colour as the outline. Let dry.

3 Using soft-peak icing of the same colour, repeat the outline and

add details like a bow or a dot design. For dot designs, pipe dots into the still-soft icing (see Baby Bootees, page 50); for bows, wait until the basic colour underneath has set.

TO MAKE THE DRESSES:

1 For full dresses outline, fill in and decorate the cookies using the same techniques as above.

2 For 2-piece outfits, outline the top and the skirt separately using soft-peak icing in two different colours.

3 Fill in the top first and let dry. Then fill in the skirt and let that dry.

4 Repeat the outlining of the cookies using the same icing, and add small details like collars, belts or bows. Let dry.

5 For dot designs, pipe dots into the still-soft icing (see Baby Bootees, page 50); for collars, belts or bows, wait until the basic colour underneath has set.

snowflake cookies

These sparkly little jewels are easy to make and will add a magical touch to any Christmas party. To turn them into strikingly original tree ornaments, simply poke a hole into the cookies before you bake them and then hang them up using lengths of satin ribbon.

FOR 6 COOKIES

300g royal icing (see page 24)

6 gingerbread cookies (see page 11) **in the shape of snowflakes**

white edible glitter

EQUIPMENT

✳ **bowls**

✳ **small palette knife**

✳ **paper piping bags** (see page 25)

1 First prepare your icing bags. Fill 1 with white soft-peak icing and 2 with white runny icing.

2 Pipe the outline of the cookie, including the design in the centre.

3 Using white runny icing, fill in the centre.

4 While still wet, drizzle white glitter generously over the icing until completely covered. Let dry.

5 Before use, shake off any excess glitter.

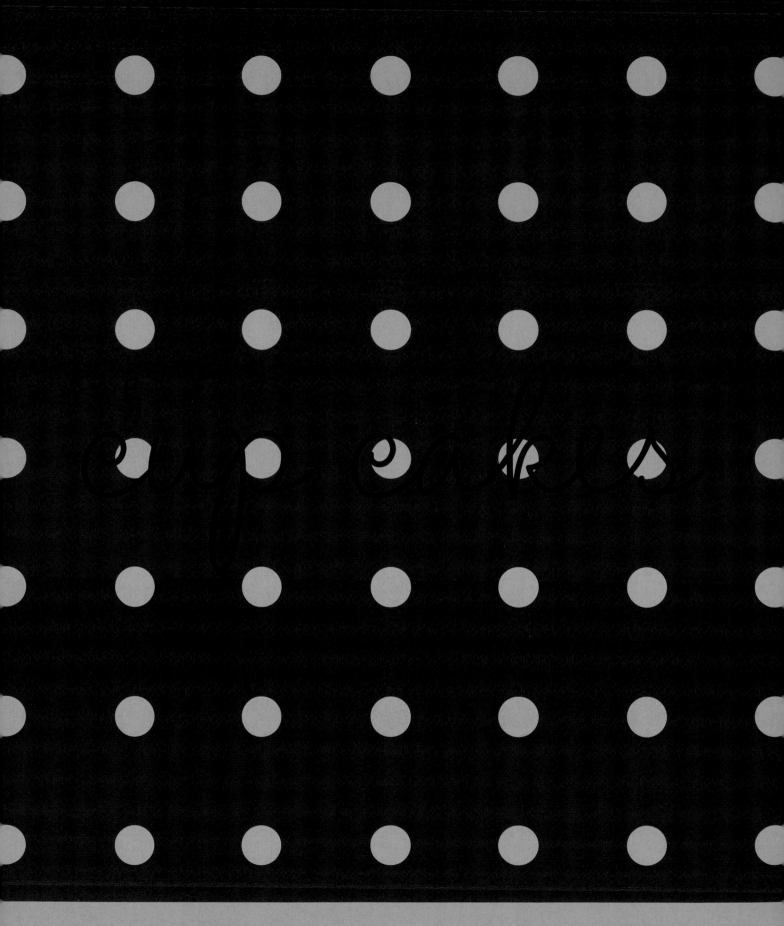

cup cakes

cup cake garden

As the name might suggest, these cup cakes may be decorated with any kind of flower you choose. Make a variety of the sugar flowers as shown on pages 26–7 (here we've used the simple 5-petal flowers only) and place one on each cake. For an attractive and original table centre-piece, you can easily arrange some of these cakes on a pretty cake stand and then bedeck them with some fresh flowers from your garden – or the florist.

FOR 25 CUP CAKES

25 pink 5-petal sugar blossoms
   (see page 26)

25 chocolate cup cakes (made using
   ½ recipe quantity basic Victoria
   sponge, see page 12, baked in silver
   paper cases)

150ml plain sugar syrup (see page 15)

250g chocolate ganache (see page 15)

100g royal icing (see page 24)

green food colour

EQUIPMENT

* pastry brush

* small palette knife

* paper piping bag (see page 25)

* scissors

1 Make the sugar blossoms a day in advance, as described on page 26.

2 Using a pastry brush, soak the tops of the cup cakes with the sugar syrup.

3 Using a small palette knife, ice the cup cakes with chocolate ganache. Let set.

4 Place one sugar blossom on top of each cup cake, fixing in place with a little drop of ganache.

5 Mix the royal icing with some green food colour and put it in the piping bag. Cut a 'V' shape in the tip of the bag and pipe some leaves around the flower (see Flower Basket Cookies, page 36).

daisy dot cup cakes

The decoration of sweet daisies, looking so pure and innocent, makes these pretty cup cakes ideal for celebrating name days or a little girl's birthday party, but they can also serve as adorable treats for people of all types and ages – especially keen gardeners.

FOR 12 CUPCAKES:
MAKE THE SUGAR DAISIES AT
LEAST ONE DAY AHEAD

200g white flower paste
   (Squires Kitchen is best)
a little white vegetable fat
icing sugar, for dusting
yellow food colour
caster sugar, for dipping
a little royal icing (see page 24)
12 vanilla cup cakes, iced with
      fondant icing (see pages 19–23)
      in pastel colours

EQUIPMENT

* small plastic board
* PME daisy cutter
* small palette knife
* foam pad
* Cel Stick or toothpick
* painter's palette
* small rolling pin
* artist's brush
* paper piping bag (see page 25)

1 Knead the paste with a little vegetable fat until smooth and pliable.

2 Roll out a walnut-sized piece of paste on a plastic board until very thin. Should it want to stick to the board, grease it lightly with the fat.

3 Press the daisy cutter firmly on the paste and cut out the shape (see 1). Carefully lift with a palette knife and lay on the foam pad.

4 Roll the Cel Stick gently back and forth over each petal as shown to shape it (see 2).

5 Dust a painter's palette with icing sugar and place the flower over one of the wells. Push the centre down gently with the end of the rolling pin (see 3).

6 Mix a small bead of flower paste with a knife tip of yellow food colour and shape to a ball. Brush lightly with water and dip in sugar. Stick in the centre of the daisy with a little water. Repeat to make 12 daisies. Let dry overnight.

DECORATE THE CUP CAKES:

7 Pipe a dot of royal icing on top of each cup cake and stick a daisy on it.

8 Finish by piping little dots of white icing all over the tops.

kaleidoscope cakes

My best 'cake mate', Anne Schultes, from Cologne in Germany, gave me this idea. She is one of the most creative, talented and inspiring cake decorators I know and she has been a great support to me throughout my career. Some time ago we decided to adopt a joint motto 'Born to bake and decorate!'. As these cakes are very graphic and their geometric designs are straightforward – however dazzling – they have proved particularly popular with male recipients, so they will make great birthday cup cakes for the man in your life.

FOR 25 CUP CAKES

25 (vanilla or lemon) cup cakes
   (made using ½ recipe quantity
basic Victoria sponge, see page 12,
   baked in silver paper cases)
150ml flavoured sugar syrup (see page 15)
100g sieved apricot jam
1.5 kg fondant icing (see page 20)
selection of food colours
300g royal icing (see page 24)

EQUIPMENT

✳ pastry brush
✳ small saucepan
✳ small palette knife
✳ bowls
✳ paper piping bags (see page 25)
✳ scissors

1 Using a pastry brush, soak the tops of the cup cakes with the sugar syrup.

2 Bring the jam to the boil in a small pan and brush a thin layer on top of each soaked cup cake, using the pastry brush.

3 Make up some fondant icing in different colours and dip the cup cakes in them, as described on page 21. Let dry.

4 Fill your piping bag with soft-peak royal icing, coloured to your choice. Pipe geometrical lines and patterns on top of the cup cakes as shown (also see the basic piping techniques on page 25).

5 Always pipe one colour first on all your cup cakes and let that dry before you pipe the next pattern in a different colour on top.

bollywood kitsch cakes

As the name suggests, the idea for these cakes came to me when Bollywood turned into high fashion and Andrew Lloyd Webber's glittering musical *Bombay Dreams* premiered, inspiring me to make these sparkling edible jewels.

FOR ABOUT 30 FONDANT FANCIES

30 fondant fancies (made as described on pages 22–3, using 1 recipe quantity basic Victoria sponge and bright pink, yellow, orange, turquoise and purple fondant icing)

15 small pink marzipan roses (see page 28)

45 small pink marzipan rosebuds (see page 28)

90 small green marzipan rose leaves (see page 28)

pink and green edible glitter

100g soft-peak royal icing (see page 24)

edible gold lustre

1 tablespoon clear alcohol (such as vodka)

EQUIPMENT

✳ about 30 golden paper cases

✳ small palette knife

✳ paper piping bags (see page 25)

✳ scissors

✳ fine artist's brush

1 Put the fondant fancies in golden paper cases.

2 Make the roses, rosebuds and leaves as described on page 28. While the marzipan is still wet, dip the flowers in the pink glitter and the leaves in the green glitter.

3 Put the soft-peak royal icing into a paper piping bag and pipe fine swirls or dots on top of the fondant fancies as shown (see 1). Let dry.

4 Mix some gold lustre to a paste with a drop of clear alcohol and use the paintbrush to colour the swirls and dots with it (see 2).

5 Stick the roses and leaves into the middle of each cake using a dab of royal icing (see 3).

hot hearts

These sparkling little heart cakes, which are very simple and easy to make, are completely adorable. Surprise the love of your life with this edible token of your devotion at a Valentine's Day dinner, or use them as treats at a wedding or engagement party.

FOR ABOUT 30

30 heart-shaped fondant fancies
   (made as described on pages 22–3,
   using red and pink fondant icing)
red and pink edible glitter
1 tablespoon clear alcohol (such as
   vodka)

EQUIPMENT

✳ about 30 silver paper cases
✳ greaseproof paper
✳ pastry brush

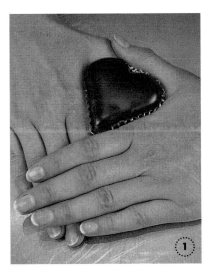

1 While the fondant icing on the fancies is still slightly wet, place each heart fancy in a silver paper case, hold between both hands as shown and push the paper case against the sides until it sticks to the cake (see 1).

2 Sprinkle a thick layer of each type of glitter on a small piece of greaseproof paper.

3 Brush each red heart thinly with the clear alcohol and dip into the red glitter (see 2); do the same with the pink hearts and the pink glitter.

christmas trees

These little dazzlers provide a modern and elegant approach to traditional festive celebrations. The soft contrast of sparkling snow-white trees on an icy pine-green background, make these cakes look effortlessly stylish. You can, of course, do the reverse to great effect.

FOR ABOUT 30

300g royal icing (see page 24)

edible white glitter

30 fondant fancies, cut into 1 x 2 inch (2.5 x 5cm) rectangles (made as described on pages 22–3, using pastel-green fondant icing)

EQUIPMENT

* sheet of cellophane
* small amount of vegetable fat
* template with small tree shapes (see page 140)
* paper piping bags (see page 25)
* small palette knife

1 Make the royal icing trees at least 2 days in advance. Place the cellophane on top of the tree template and rub a very thin layer of vegetable fat over it with your hand so that the icing won't stick to it.

2 Fill 1 piping bag with soft-peak white royal icing and 1 bag with runny white royal icing.

3 Using the soft-peak icing, first pipe the outlines of the trees on the cellophane (see 1).

4 Fill the centres of the trees with the runny icing (see 2) and, while still wet, sprinkle white glitter over the trees (see 3).

5 Let dry in a warm place for 2 days.

6 Once they are dry, lift them from the cellophane with a palette knife and stick them on top of the fondant fancies using a dot of royal icing.

ruffle rose cup cakes

I saw this gorgeously girly cakestand in a department store while I was on a trip to New York, and I just had to have it. Here its romantic ruffle design provides the perfect setting for my wild rose cup cakes, which were inspired by it.

FOR ABOUT 25 CUP CAKES

25 vanilla cup cakes (made using ½ recipe quantity basic Victoria sponge, see page 12, baked in white paper cases)

150ml vanilla sugar syrup (see page 15)

500g vanilla buttercream (see page 14)

75 small dusky pink marzipan roses (3 per cup cake, see page 28)

150 small moss-green marzipan leaves (6 per cup cake, see page 28)

EQUIPMENT

✳ pastry brush
✳ small palette knife

1 Using the pastry brush, soak the tops of the cup cakes with the sugar syrup.

2 Using the palette knife, cover the tops with the buttercream.

3 Place the roses and the leaves on top of the cakes, pressing them slightly into the buttercream to fix them in place.

4 Ideally, arrange them on a beautiful old-fashioned cakestand.

butterfly fancies

If you want to add a real touch of magic to your party, you can't go wrong with these delicate butterfly fancies. Don't they just look as if they want to fly away? Be careful, though, you'd better keep an eye on them…Perhaps it would be better to eat them first.

FOR ABOUT 25 FANCIES

small amount of vegetable fat

food colours (pink, orange, yellow and blue)

350g royal icing (see page 24)

25 small fondant fancies, 1½ inch (4cm) square (made as described on pages 22–3 – you will need about ½ sheet of basic Victoria sponge – using fondant icing in several different candy colours)

EQUIPMENT

✳ sheet of cellophane

✳ butterfly templates (see page 140–1)

✳ paper piping bags (see page 25)

✳ thin cardboard

✳ greaseproof paper

✳ scissors

✳ small palette knife

✳ 25 silver cup cases

Prepare the butterflies at least 2 days in advance. Place the cellophane on top of the butterfly templates and rub a very thin layer of vegetable fat on top with your hands to prevent the icing sticking.

TO MAKE THE YELLOW BUTTERFLY:

1 Mix your colours and prepare your piping bags. You will need 1 piping bag filled with soft-peak yellow icing, another with soft-peak pale-blue icing, and a third with runny yellow icing.

2 Using the soft-peak yellow icing, pipe the outline of the butterfly.

3 Using the runny yellow icing, fill the top wings and let them dry.

4 Using the same icing, fill the bottom wings and let dry.

5 Using soft-peak pale-blue icing, pipe the little blue dots on top as shown.

TO MAKE THE BLUE BUTTERFLY:

1 Mix your colours and prepare your piping bags. You will need 1 bag filled with soft-peak blue icing, another with soft-peak green (yellow plus blue) icing, and a third with runny blue icing.

2 Using the soft-peak blue icing, pipe the outline of the butterfly.

3 Using the runny blue icing, fill the top wings and let them dry.

4 Using the same icing, fill the bottom wings and let dry.

5 Using soft-peak blue icing, pipe the little blue dots on top as shown.

TO MAKE THE GREEN BUTTERFLY:

1 Mix your colours and prepare your icing bags. You will need 1 piping bag filled with soft-peak bright-green icing, another with runny bright-green icing and a third with runny light-green icing.

2 Using the soft-peak bright-green icing, pipe the outline of the butterfly.

3 Using the runny bright-green icing, fill the top wings and let them dry.

4 Using the runny light-green icing, fill the bottom wings and let dry.

TO MAKE THE PINK BUTTERFLY:

1 Mix your colours and prepare your icing bags. You will need 1 piping bag filled with soft-peak pale-pink icing, another with runny pale-pink icing and a third with runny bright-pink icing.

2 Using the pale-pink soft-peak icing, pipe the outline of the butterfly.

3 Using the same icing, pipe a parallel line just inside the wing outline, leaving a small border.

4 Using the runny pale-pink icing, fill the gap between these outlines.

5 Using the runny bright-pink icing, fill the centres. Let dry.

TO MAKE THE ORANGE BUTTERFLY:

1 Mix your colours and prepare your icing bags. You will need 1 piping bag filled with soft-peak yellow icing, another with runny yellow icing and a third with runny orange icing.

2 Using the yellow soft-peak icing, pipe the outline of the butterfly.

3 Using the same icing, pipe an inner line as shown outline, leaving a border.

4 Using the runny orange icing, fill the main centres of the wings. Let dry.

5 Using the runny yellow icing, fill the outside border and making the dots. Let dry.

TO FINISH ALL THE BUTTERFLIES:

1 Pipe a couple of feelers for each butterfly in a matching colour on a piece of greaseproof paper.

2 Let everything dry and set for at least 2 days in a warm dry place.

3 Fold some pieces of thin cardboard to a 'V' shape to support the wings when sticking them together and line with a piece of folded greaseproof paper (see 1).

4 Pipe a small line of royal icing in a colour matching the butterfly into the fold of the paper (see 2). Lift the wings with the small palette knife and place them in position on either side of the 'V' shape (see 3). Let the butterflies dry in position for at least 3 hours.

5 Put the fondant fancies in silver cup cases and stick a butterfly on top of each with a dot of stiff-peak royal icing (see 4 and 5).

6 Using soft-peak icing in appropriate colours, pipe a head and a body in the middle between the wings (see 6) and stick two feelers carefully into the head (see 7).

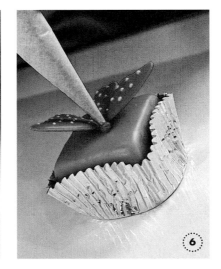
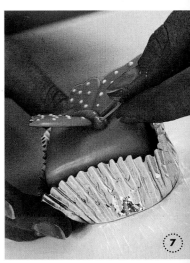

miniature cakes

pansy pots

My parents, both dedicated hobby gardeners, were undoubtedly the inspiration for these adorable little cakes, as pansies are high on their list of favourite flowers. Whenever I go back home in spring, our garden is just full of their brilliant colours. It's no surprise, then, that I felt compelled to turn their passion into sweet treats as gifts for them. Make these cakes at least a day before you need them. The pansy flowers can be made well in advance, as they last for weeks.

FOR 12 CAKES

butter and flour for lining the moulds

¼ recipe quantity chocolate sponge mixture (see page 10)

100ml plain sugar syrup (see page 15)

500g white sugar paste

food colours (brown, orange, pink, yellow, violet, moss green)

1 teaspoon tylo powder (see step 6)

300g white flower paste

small amount of white vegetable fat

50g sieved apricot jam

250g chocolate-flavoured sugar paste

100g royal icing (see page 24)

EQUIPMENT

* 12 timbale moulds
* wire cooling rack
* pastry brush
* cling film
* small plastic board
* pansy petal and leaf cutters
* foam pad
* bone tool
* fine artist's brush
* small painter's palette
* black edible ink pen
* small rolling pin
* small kitchen knife
* leaf veining mat
* paper piping bag (page 25)

1 To bake the sponges: preheat the oven to 180°C, gas4. Grease 12 timbale moulds with butter and then dust them with flour, shaking out excess.

2 Make the sponge mixture as described on page 10 and then spoon it into the prepared timbale moulds just enough to half fill them only.

3 Bake in the preheated oven for about 15 minutes. Allow the cakes to cool a little on a wire rack and then turn them out of their moulds (see 1 overleaf).

4 Make the flowerpots: once the sponge cakes are cool, soak their tops with the sugar syrup using a pastry brush, wrap them in cling film and chill for at least 2 hours to firm them up.

5 Mix the white sugar paste with some brown and orange food colour until you achieve a nice terracotta colour.

6 Mix in the tylo powder (this is a hardening agent and will also help to make the paste more flexible and stable), wrap in cling film and allow the paste to rest for at least half an hour.

7 While the paste is resting, make the pansy flowers. Divide the white

flower paste into 7 pieces. Keep 1 white and colour the remaining pieces with yellow, moss green and 2 different shades of pink and violet. Wrap the ones you aren't going to use immediately in cling film to prevent them from drying out.

8 Rub a thin layer of white vegetable fat over a plastic board to prevent the flower paste from sticking to it.

9 Roll out one colour of paste very thinly and, using a pansy petal cutter, cut out the petals. For one blossom you will need 2 large and 2 small teardrop-shaped petals and 1 large base petal as shown.

10 Place the petals on the foam pad and smooth the edges by using the bone tool (see 4).

11 Arrange the petals into a flower by placing the 2 small petals next to each other, slightly overlapping, and stick them together by brushing the sides where they touch with a little bit of water. Place the 2 large petals to the left and to the right below the small petals, also overlapping and touching the sides. Use a little water to stick them to the small petals. Finally stick on the large base petal with a little bit of water (see 5) and push a little well into the centre, using the end of a brush or a pointed flower tool (see 6).

12 Place the flower into the well of a small painter's palette to let it dry (see 7). Repeat the procedure

for all the flowers; you will need 6 flowers per pot.

13 Depending on the thickness of your paste, let them dry for at least 2–4 hours.

14 Once they are dry, paint some fine black lines into the centre using a black edible ink pen.

15 When the sponges are chilled, bring the jam to the boil in a small pan, turn the sponges upside down and brush sides and tops with jam.

16 Roll out the terracotta paste to about ⅛ inch (3mm) thick and lay it over the upside-down sponges. Using a kitchen knife, trim off the excess paste and let the iced cakes set for at least 4 hours, until the paste feels firm to the touch (see 1).

17 Turn the cakes back over. Roll out some more of the terracotta paste to the same thickness as before and cut out 12 strips each ½ inch (1cm) wide and about 6 inches (15cm) long (they dry out very quickly, so it is best to work on 3 or 4 at a time).

18 Brush the top edge of each pot with a little bit of water and stick the terracotta strip around it (see 2). If the strip is too long, trim off the excess with a small knife.

19 Roll a piece of chocolate-flavoured sugar paste into a ball and flatten it to a slight dome shape large enough to cover the sponge still showing inside the pot.

20 Brush with hot jam and stick the paste on top (see 3).

21 Before sticking the flowers on top of the pot, make the pansy leaves. Mix some of the flower paste with moss-green food colour and roll it out very thinly.

22 Cut out the leaves using a metal leaf cutter and place them on the foam pad.

23 Use the bone tool to smooth the edges and the veining mat to give them veins (see 8).

24 Stick the flowers and leaves on top of the flowerpots with little dabs of royal icing. While they are still soft, shape the leaves and make sure you have hardly any gaps between the flowers and the leaves (see 9).

MAKING THE PANSY POTS

mini tea rose wedding cakes

Miniature wedding cakes provide a modern twist to the traditional large cake and are ideal for smaller wedding receptions. Instead of having one large cake to cut, the bride and groom can serve individual cakes to each of their guests. This particular cake is inspired by the lovely ceramic artistry of the tea set on which it is served. Make the cake at least a day in advance. The flowers can be made well before you need them, as they will last for weeks.

FOR 6 CAKES

1 sheet of sponge cake, 12 x 16 inches (30 x 40cm), using 1 recipe quantity of basic Victoria sponge mixture, flavoured and soaked to your choice (see page 12)

100g sieved apricot jam

icing sugar for dusting

500g white sugar paste

50g sugar paste

violet food colour

50g royal icing (see page 24)

edible gold lustre powder

1 teaspoon clear alcohol (such as vodka)

30 mini roses made from sugar paste coloured dusky pink (see pages 26–9)

36 rose leaves made from moss-green sugar paste (see pages 26–9)

EQUIPMENT

* cling film
* round pastry cutters, 3 inch (7.5cm) and 1½ inch (3.5cm) diameter
* small saucepan
* pastry brush
* small rolling pin
* ¼ inch (5mm) guide sticks
* 2 cake smoothers
* small kitchen knife
* greaseproof paper
* small plastic board
* miniature blossom cutter
* bone tool
* paper piping bags (see page 25)
* fine artist's brush

1 Wrap the soaked sheet of sponge in cling film and chill for about 2 hours until firm.iuu

2 Using 3 inch (7.5cm) and 1½ inch (3.5cm) round pastry cutters, cut out 6 rounds in each size from the firmed-up sponge.

3 Bring the jam to the boil in a small pan and, using a pastry brush, brush each round all over with the hot jam.

4 On a work surface dusted with icing sugar, roll out the white sugar paste to ¼ inch (5mm) thick using guide sticks and cover each of the rounds with the paste, as described on page 17.

5 Use the cake smoothers to straighten the sides and tops of each of the cakes.

6 Trim off excess paste using a small kitchen knife, place the cakes on a sheet of greaseproof paper and let set for a day.

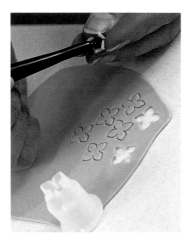

7 Make the little lilac blossoms by mixing the sugar paste with a little bit of violet food colour. Roll it out thinly on a plastic board dusted with icing sugar. Cut out the blossoms using a mini blossom cutter and shape them with a bone tool as shown. Let dry overnight.

8 Pipe a small dot of royal icing in the centre of each of the large cakes and then place a small cake on top.

9 Pipe a border (see page 25) around the base of each tier and let it dry.

10 Mix some gold lustre powder to a paste with a little bit of clear alcohol and paint the piped border using a fine artist's brush.

11 Stick the lilac blossoms, mini roses and leaves on top of the cake with little dabs of royal icing.

treasure boxes

These little sugar boxes make exclusive keepsakes for special occasions. The design is inspired by my favourite tableware, Follement by Christian Lacroix. Finished with lavishly formed golden handles, they look more like treasure boxes. You need good piping skills and some patience to make them. If you're worried that these designs are a bit too hard for you, keep the look simple. Dust the entire box with one colour and use a marzipan rose (see page 29) for the handle.

FOR 6 BOXES
MAKE THE BOXES AT LEAST 3 DAYS BEFORE YOU NEED THEM

300g white sugar paste

1 teaspoon Tylo Powder (see page 83)

1 egg white

icing sugar for dusting

a little vegetable fat

edible lustre powders (gold, pink blue, green and yellow)

a little clear alcohol, such as vodka or gin

a little royal icing (see page 24)

EQUIPMENT

❋ cling film

❋ round bottle or tin

❋ piece of cardboard

❋ small rolling pin

❋ ¼ inch (5mm) guide sticks

❋ small kitchen knife

❋ several fine artist's brushes

❋ tray

❋ round pastry cutters

❋ paper piping bags (see page 25)

1 Mix the sugar paste with the Tylo Powder to make a modelling paste. Wrap in cling film and allow to rest for 15 minutes.

2 Choose a bottle that would make a good template. Cut a rectangular piece of cardboard about 2½ inches (6cm) wide and long enough to wrap around the bottle. Using guide sticks, roll a piece of paste out to a thickness of ⅛ inch (3mm) and, using the template, cut out a strip that size (see 1 overleaf). Brush the end of the strip lightly with egg white. Dust the paste with icing sugar and wrap around the bottle (see 2 overleaf). Carefully squeeze the ends together to stick. Move to a tray dusted with icing sugar. Carefully remove the bottle and leave the cylinder to dry overnight.

3 To make the lid, roll another piece of modelling paste out to the same thickness and use a suitably sized cutter to stamp out a lid. Let dry on the tray overnight.

4 To make the handles, roll a piece of paste into a small sausage and shape it into swirls and curls. Let dry overnight.

5 Next day, roll out a small piece of paste as before. Brush the edge of one end of the paste cylinder with a little egg white and place firmly on the paste so it sticks. With a sharp knife, cut around the edge to leave the new base in place (see 3). Place the box, bottom side down, on a tray that has been dusted with icing sugar and let dry overnight.

6 Next day, fill a piping bag with soft-peak royal icing and pipe swirls and waves on the box and the lid (see 4). Let dry for an hour.

7 Once dry, using a fine brush, apply a thin layer of vegetable fat to parts you want to colour. Using another clean dry brush, dust these with the edible lustre powder (see 5).

8 Mix a small amount of gold powder to a paste with a drop of alcohol. Use to paint the piped lines and the handle (see 6).

9 Brush the handles with a little of the fat and dust with lustre powder using a thick artist's brush (see 6).

10 Pipe a dot of royal icing in the middle of the lid and stick the handle on top. Let dry for 2 hours.

swirly whirly cakes

These crazy little swirly party cakes were inspired by an ultra-cool piece of fabric which grabbed my eye in the window of a shop near my house. I often find that fabrics, wallpapers and china services provide a fabulous source of inspiration. I just love to wander through interiors and ceramics shops in hope of finding something special that will spark off a new idea. These are nice and easy to do for beginners – or even for getting the children to help.

FOR ABOUT 12–15 CAKES

1 sheet of chocolate sponge 12 x16 inches (30 x 40cm), using 1 recipe quantity of basic Victoria sponge mixture (see page 12)

250ml sugar syrup, flavoured to your choice (see page 15)

250g chocolate ganache (see page 15)

icing sugar for dusting

750g chocolate-flavoured sugar paste

300g white sugar paste

selection of food colours

100g soft-peak royal icing (see page 24)

EQUIPMENT

* bread knife and small kitchen knife
* pastry brush
* cling film
* selection of round pastry cutters
* small palette knife
* rolling pin
* ¼ inch (5mm) guide sticks
* 2 cake smoothers
* selection of different-coloured satin ribbon,10mm wide
* scissors

1 Trim the sponge and soak it with the syrup using a pastry brush. Wrap in cling film and chill for about 2 hours until firm.

2 Once it is firm, use the pastry cutters to cut out a variety of round miniature cakes in different sizes.

3 Using a palette knife, cover each cake thinly with the chocolate ganache.

4 On a surface dusted with icing sugar, roll out the chocolate paste using the rolling pin and the guide sticks.

5 Cover each cake with the paste as described on page 17 and trim off the excess with a kitchen knife.

6 Use the cake smoothers to straighten the sides and the top of the cakes.

7 Mix the white sugar paste with different colours as you require. Roll out each colour until very thin and cut out different rings and circles using the pastry cutters.

8 Arrange these on top of the cakes to make different designs, using a bit of royal icing to stick the paste on the cake.

9 Outline a few rings with white royal icing.

10 Cut pieces of satin ribbon in colours that match the decoration and stick them around the base of each cake with little dabs of royal icing.

miniature wedding cake

As a specialist in making wedding cakes, I have noticed right from my very first commissions that although brides these days are still looking for something traditional, more and more they want a cake with an unusual twist to it. As this idea provides both a cutting cake and individual cakes that can be used as favours at the same time, it is no surprise that it has become one of my bestsellers. Another advantage of this cake is that you can offer your guests a choice of different cake flavours.

It is best to make as much of this as possible in advance: try to start making the top tier and the miniature cakes 2 days ahead, the sugar flowers at least 1 day ahead and the chocolate ganache half a day.

FOR ABOUT 80 MINIATURE CAKES AND ONE 6 INCH (15CM) TOP TIER

1 sheet of orange-flavoured sponge cake, 12 x 16 inches (30 x 40 cm), using 1 recipe quantity of basic Victoria sponge mixture (see page 12)

1 sheet of lemon-flavoured sponge cake, 12 x 16 inches (30 x 40 cm), using 1 recipe quantity of basic Victoria sponge mixture (see page 12)

6 inch (15cm) round chocolate sponge cake, using ½ recipe quantity basic Victoria sponge mixture (see page 12)

150ml sugar syrup (see page 15) flavoured with finely grated orange zest and juice and Grand Marnier

100g orange marmalade

150g orange-flavoured buttercream (see page 14)

150ml sugar syrup (see page 15) flavoured with finely grated lemon zest, lemon juice and Limoncello

150g lemon curd (I use best-quality bought)

150g lemon-flavoured buttercream (see page 14)

100ml plain sugar syrup (see page 15)

250g chocolate ganache (see page 15), flavoured with peppermint liqueur

450g white marzipan

5kg white sugar paste

150g sieved apricot jam

250g royal icing (see page 24)

icing sugar for dusting

80 5-petal flowers (see pages 26–7) in two different shades of pink

green food colour

EQUIPMENT

* large serrated knife
* pastry brush
* cling film
* 6 inch (15cm) round cake board
* round pastry cutter, 2 inch (5cm) diameter
* 2 large trays
* large rolling pin
* ¼ inch (5mm) guide sticks
* 15m satin ribbon, 15mm thick, in two shades of pink
* small saucepan
* kitchen knife
* cake smoothers
* greaseproof paper
* paper piping bag (see page 25)
* 4-tier Perspex cake stand (try to hire one from a local cake-maker)
* 25 bright pink fresh roses and 25 pale pink fresh roses, plus some more petals, to decorate

TO FILL THE CAKES:

1 Once your sponge cakes are cool, trim the top crust off each of them using a large serrated knife.

2 For the orange cakes, slice the sheet of orange sponge in half and soak the tops of both layers with the orange-flavoured sugar syrup.

3 Spread one layer with orange marmalade then with orange buttercream, and sandwich the other on top. Wrap in cling film and chill for at least an hour until firm.

4 For the lemon cakes, slice the sheet of lemon sponge in half and soak the tops of both layers with the lemon-flavoured sugar syrup.

5 Spread one layer with lemon curd, then with lemon buttercream and sandwich the other on top. Wrap in cling film and chill for at least an hour until firm.

6 For the 6 inch (15cm) top tier, slice the round chocolate sponge into 3 layers and soak each one with the plain sugar syrup.

7 Layer the sponges with the peppermint-flavoured chocolate ganache. Chill for at least 1 hour until the ganache has set.

8 Once set, stick the chocolate cake on to a 6 inch (15cm) round cake board with a dab of the ganache and coat it with ganache once more until even and smooth. Chill again.

9 Take the chilled orange and lemon sponge out of the fridge and cut out rounds from them using a 2 inch (5cm) diameter pastry cutter. Each sheet should produce about 40. Place them on a tray, wrap in cling film and chill again until needed.

TO DECORATE THE CAKES:

10 For the top tier: remove the chocolate cake from the fridge and cover it in thin coat of chocolate ganache to help the marzipan stick.

11 Cover the cake with the marzipan and then 500g of the white sugar paste as described on page 17. Let everything set for 1 day.

12 Once set, lay some dark-pink satin ribbon around the sides and fix in place with a dot of royal icing.

13 For the miniature cakes: bring the apricot jam to the boil in a small pan. Remove the little cakes from the fridge and brush the tops and the sides with the jam, using a pastry brush.

14 On a surface dusted with icing sugar, roll out some of the white sugar paste, using ¼ inch (5mm) guide sticks.

15 Cover each cake with the sugar paste and trim off excess. Use cake smoothers to smooth the top and the sides. Place the cakes on a tray lined with greaseproof paper and let set overnight.

16 Once set, attach a small piece of satin ribbon around the base of each tier with a dab of royal icing. Use one shade for each flavour, so you will be able to differentiate the cake types when serving them.

17 Stick a 5-petal flower in a shade matching that of the ribbon on top of each cake with a dab of icing.

18 Mix a little bit of royal icing with some green food colour, snip the tip of a paper icing bag in a 'V' shape and pipe small leaves around each flower.

ARRANGING THE CAKES:

19 Place the 6 inch (15cm) cake on the top tier of a cake stand. Arrange the little cakes on the tiers below, leaving some gaps for fresh roses.

20 Arrange some fresh roses and petals all over the cake stand and the top tier.

chocolate canapés

I wanted to create a smart, cosmopolitan cake design that could be served as both a sweet canapé at cocktail parties and a petit four after dinner. I think these little stripy squares do the trick. They are totally stylish and look best when on a simple plate. I like to think that Paul Smith might offer these at one of his fashion shows. Serve them on the day they are made.

MAKES 120 SQUARES
(60 of each colour combination)

1 sheet of sponge cake, 12 x 16 inches (30 x 40cm), using 1 recipe quantity basic Victoria sponge mixture, flavoured and soaked to your choice (see page 12)

150ml plain sugar syrup (see page 15)

150g chocolate ganache (see page 15), flavoured with peppermint liqueur

400g white sugar paste

food colours (yellow, orange, blue)

200g chocolate-flavoured sugar paste

icing sugar for dusting

EQUIPMENT
* cling film
* large palette knife
* small rolling pin
* kitchen knife
* small plastic board

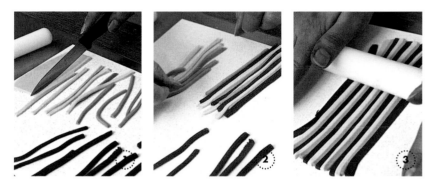

1 Wrap the soaked sponge in cling film and chill for 2 hours until firm.

2 Once firm, spread the sponge with a thin layer of chocolate ganache, using a large palette knife.

3 Divide the white sugar paste into 4 equal parts and colour them in yellow, orange, blue and green (use a mixture of yellow and blue to achieve this last colour).

4 Roll out the chocolate paste to ¼ inch (5mm) thick and cut into thin strips about ⅛ inch (2–3mm) wide. Repeat with coloured pastes (see 1).

5 The colour combinations shown are chocolate, orange and yellow, and chocolate, green and blue, but it is up to you how you would like to arrange them. Choose 2 different colour combinations. Cut the sponge sheet in half and cover each half with a different colour. Do one at a time by arranging the stripes in alternating colours next to each other on a plastic board or surface dusted with icing sugar (see 2). Use a rolling pin to roll them out very thinly so the paste is large enough to cover half of the sponge sheet. By rolling them out close to each other, the strips will stick together (see 3).

6 Trim off the edges of the sponge and the paste so that you end up with clean and straight sides.

7 Cut each sheet into 1 inch (2.5cm) squares using a damp sharp kitchen knife.

stripy rose cakes

Smart stripes and candy pink are more fashionable than ever, and help turn these pretty pastries into couture cakes. I recently made these cakes for a friend and, for a change, decorated them with stripes in vivid rainbow colours – they were a great hit.

FOR ABOUT 15
MAKE THESE AT LEAST A DAY
IN ADVANCE

½ sheet of sponge cake, 12 x 16 inches (30 x 40cm), using 1 recipe quantity of basic Victoria sponge mixture, flavoured, soaked and filled to your choice (see pages 12–16)

150g sieved apricot jam

icing sugar for dusting

750g white sugar paste

250g royal icing (see page 24)

pink food colour

15 pink sugar paste roses with green calyxes (see page 28)

EQUIPMENT

* cling film
* 2 inch (5cm) round pastry cutter
* small saucepan
* pastry brush
* small rolling pin
* ¼ inch (5mm) guide sticks
* small kitchen knife
* 2 cake smoothers
* greaseproof paper
* small palette knife
* paper piping bags (see page 25)

1 Wrap the soaked and filled sheet of sponge in cling film and chill for about 2 hours until firm.

2 Using a 2 inch (5cm) round pastry cutter, cut out about 15 circles.

3 Bring the apricot jam to the boil in a small pan and, using a pastry brush, brush each cake all over with the jam.

4 On a surface dusted with icing sugar, roll out the sugar paste to ¼ inch (5mm) thick using guide sticks. Cover each cake with the paste as described on page 17.

5 Trim off the excess paste using a small kitchen knife.

6 Use the cake smoothers to straighten the sides and top of the cakes. Place on a sheet of grease-proof paper and let dry for 1 day.

7 Once the icing has set firm, fill one piping bag with soft-peak icing in pastel pink and another with soft-peak icing in bright pink.

8 Pipe lines as shown, starting at the top in the centre, lifting the bag and bringing it slowly down to the bottom of the cake. Touch the end point and stop piping (see Basic Piping Techniques on page 25.) Pipe one line next to the other in alternating colours, keeping the lines nice and straight.

9 Finish the lines by piping small dots in the same colours along the base.

10 Place a sugar paste rose on top of each cake and stick it on with a dab of royal icing.

'stripes and candy pink are more fashionable than ever'

fantasy cake slices

When I first came to London to begin studying pâtisserie, I quickly learned all about the delightful English tradition of afternoon tea. Although I loved the concept right from the start, I have always felt that it needed some fresh ideas. These fantasy slices combine simple and yummy cakes with charming and playful designs that are guaranteed to be a success at your next tea party. The cakes are ideal for mixing and matching different flavours and colours, so feel free to experiment a little bit and create your own favourites.

There may seem an awful lot of steps to this, but it is one of those methods that looks much more complicated than it actually is – it is more or less the same procedure done three times with subtle differences.

FOR 18 SLICES

1 sheet of vanilla sponge cake, 12 x 16 inches (30 x 40 cm), using 1 recipe quantity of basic Victoria sponge mixture (see page 12)

1 sheet of chocolate sponge, 12 x 16 inches (30 x 40 cm), using 1 recipe quantity of basic Victoria sponge mixture (see page 12)

1 sheet of pink sponge, 12 x 16 inches (30 x 40 cm), using 1 recipe quantity of basic Victoria sponge mixture (see page 12, just adding a drop of pink food colour to the sponge mix before baking)

300ml sugar syrup (see page 15)

450g vanilla buttercream (see page 14)

500g white sugar paste

food colours (yellow, pink and green)

icing sugar for dusting

250g chocolate-flavoured sugar paste

selection of 3 different sugar flowers, such as daffodils, 5-petal flowers and pansies (see page 27, you will need 18 flowers, i.e. 6 of each)

EQUIPMENT

* large serrated knife
* large plain knife
* pastry brush
* large palette knife
* cling film
* large rolling pin
* ¼ inch (5mm) guide sticks
* 2 cake smoother
* paper piping bags (see page 25)

1 Trim the crusts off your sponges using a large serrated knife.

2 Cut each sponge into 3 equal rectangles, so that you have 3 white, 3 pink and 3 brown rectangles of sponge.

TO MAKE THE YELLOW SLAB:

1 You need 2 layers of pink sponge and 1 of white. Starting with a pink layer, soak the top with sugar syrup and spread it with buttercream, using a large palette knife.

2 Place the white layer on top, soak the top with sugar syrup and spread it with buttercream as before.

3 Place the remaining pink layer on top and soak it with sugar syrup.

4 Now trim the long sides of the slabs neatly, using a serrated knife.

5 Cover the whole slab with a coat of buttercream, but don't cover the ends. Chill for about 1 hour until the buttercream has set.

6 While that is chilling, mix the white sugar paste with a little bit of yellow food colour until pastel yellow. Keep it covered in cling film until use.

7 Once the buttercream has set, roll out the sugar paste on a surface dusted with icing sugar using a rolling pin and ¼ inch (5mm) guide sticks.

8 Apply a thin layer of buttercream on the top and sides of the slab as before to make the icing stick, and cover it with the paste (see page 17).

9 Trim off the excess icing with a small knife and smooth the top and the sides with the cake smoothers.

10 Now cut off the ends of the slab with a sharp knife, so that you can see the beautiful layering of the different-coloured sponges.

11 Slice the slab into 6 equal pieces, making sure you wipe the blade of the knife after each slice for a clean finish.

12 Now arrange a pink 5-petal flower on top of each slice, sticking it in place with a dab of royal icing.

13 Finish the look by adding little green leaves and curls to the flowers, following the same techniques as for the Bollywood Heart Lollies on page 35 and repeating the same design on each slice.

TO MAKE THE PINK SLAB:

1 You need 2 layers of white sponge and 1 of pink. Start with a white layer, soak the top with sugar syrup and spread it with buttercream, using the palette knife.

2 Place the pink layer on top, soak the top with sugar syrup and spread with buttercream as before.

3 Place the remaining white layer on top and soak it with sugar syrup.

4 Now trim the long sides of the slabs neatly, using a serrated knife.

5 Cover the whole slab with a coat of buttercream, but don't cover the ends. Chill for about 1 hour until the buttercream has set.

6 While that is chilling, mix the sugar paste with a little bit of pink food colour until pastel pink. Keep it covered in cling film until use.

7 Continue coating with buttercream, covering with the sugar paste, trimming etc., as with the yellow slab until you have the 6 equal pieces.

8 Now arrange a pansy on top of each slice, sticking it in place with a dab of royal icing.

9 Finish the look by adding little green leaves and curls to the flowers in the same way and repeating the same design on each slice.

TO MAKE THE BROWN SLAB:
1 You need 2 layers of chocolate sponge (you will have one left over to give to the kids) and 1 of pink. Starting with a chocolate layer, soak the top with sugar syrup and spread it with buttercream, using the palette knife.

2 Place the pink layer on top, soak the top with sugar syrup and spread it with buttercream as before.

3 Place the remaining chocolate layer on top and soak it with sugar syrup.

4 Now trim the long sides of the slabs neatly, using a serrated knife.

5 Cover the whole slab with a coat of buttercream, but don't cover the ends. Chill for about 1 hour until the buttercream has set.

6 Continue coating with buttercream, covering with the sugar paste (this time the chocolate-flavoured sugar paste), trimming etc., as with the yellow and pink slabs until you have the 6 equal pieces.

7 Now arrange a daffodil on top of each slice, sticking it in place with a dab of royal icing.

8 Finish the look by adding little green leaves and curls to the flowers in the same way, repeating the same design on each slice.

large cakes

Valentine's heart

It is easy to make a simple heart-shaped cake look very special indeed. The romantic floral border cascading down the sides of the cake makes a striking frame for a personal message or someone's name on top, so it could be used as a billet-doux for any sort of romantic occasion. Make this cake at least one day in advance.

FOR AN 8 INCH (20CM) CAKE
(about 25 party portions)

750g pastel-pink sugar paste

300g royal icing (see page 24)

two 8 inch (20cm) round sponge cakes, using 1 recipe quantity of basic Victoria sponge mixture, flavoured to your choice (see page 12)

150ml sugar syrup (see page 15), flavoured to your choice

250g chosen filling (buttercream, see page 14, or chocolate ganache, see page 15)

icing sugar for dusting

600g white marzipan

2 tablespoons clear alcohol (such as vodka)

selection of food colours

EQUIPMENT

✳ 12 inch (30cm) round or heart-shaped thick cake board

✳ pink satin ribbon, 15mm thick

✳ flower nail

✳ greaseproof paper

✳ metal piping nozzles for flower-making (see page 26)

✳ paper piping bags (see page 25)

✳ large serrated knife

✳ large palette knife

✳ 8 inch (20cm) heart-shaped cake board

✳ pastry brush

✳ rolling pin

✳ ¼ inch (5mm) guide sticks

✳ kitchen knife

✳ 2 cake smoothers

✳ tilting turntable

1 Cover the 12 inch (30cm) thick cake board with 150g of the pink sugar paste and the ribbon, following the instructions on page 17. Let set overnight.

2 Using the flower nail lined with pieces of greaseproof paper, royal icing and a selection of different piping nozzles, make a selection of sugar flowers, enough to cover the sides of your cake, as described on page 27. Leave to dry overnight.

3 Trim the top crust off both sponges using a serrated knife. Cut 2 heart shapes out of the sponge using the 8 inch (20cm) heart-shaped cake board as a template.

4 Soak and layer the 2 heart-shaped sponges with your chosen filling.

5 Coat the outside of the cake with the same filling and chill for at least 2 hours.

6 Once chilled, give the cake another coat of ganache or buttercream to make the marzipan stick to the cake.

7 On a surface dusted with icing sugar, roll the marzipan out between ¼ inch (5mm) guide sticks using a large rolling pin.

8 Using the rolling pin to help you, lay the marzipan over the top of the cake and push it down the side. Trim away the excess with a knife.

9 Use the cake smoothers to make the top and sides nice and even. Let set overnight.

10 Brush the outside of the marzipanned cake with a little bit of alcohol to make the sugar paste stick to the marzipan.

11 Cover the cake with the rest of the sugar paste following the same technique as for the marzipan. Let everything harden overnight.

12 Once hardened, pipe a dot of icing in the centre of the prepared thick cake board and place the cake on top. Let it set for 1 hour to make sure the cake sticks firmly to the board.

13 Prepare 3 piping bags filled with soft-peak royal icing in 3 different shades of pink.

14 Place the cake, on its board, on top of a tilting turntable. Tilt it slightly to the side away from you and then start piping lines down the sides, starting from the top edge down to the bottom edge and alternating the three shades. (See 1 and Basic Piping Techniques on page 25.)

15 Pipe a border of matching dots along the bottom of the cake (see 2).

16 Arrange the sugar flowers along the top edge to form a frame around the heart shape, using royal icing to stick the flowers in place (see 3).

17 Fill another piping bag with green stiff-peak royal icing and pipe a couple of green leaves between the flowers, as described on page 35.

three-column wedding cake

This is a rather unconventional version of a classic wedding cake, in that the different tiers are placed next to each other instead of being stacked on top of one another. The elegant dot design is very easy to accomplish and gives this cake its romantic charm. Decorating cakes with fresh flowers has become very popular and the beautiful cascading roses adorning my cake here were kindly arranged by one of London's top floral designers, Rob Van Helden, whose glamorous creations are second to none. Your florist should be able to supply the oasis dome shape holders. Alternatively, just ask them to arrange the flowers for you. Make sure the roses have not been treated with any chemicals as they come in contact with the cake. Make this cake at least three days in advance.

FOR ABOUT 100 PORTIONS

3.5kg white sugar paste

food colours (pink, orange, yellow)

6 sheets of sponge cake, 12 x 16 inches (30 x 40cm), each using 1 recipe quantity of basic Victoria sponge mixture, flavoured to your choice (see page 12)

500ml sugar syrup (see page 15), flavoured to your choice

1.5kg buttercream (see page 14) or other filling of your choice

icing sugar for dusting

3kg white marzipan

500g royal icing (see page 24)

a little clear alcohol, such as vodka

EQUIPMENT

* cling film
* 20 inch (50cm) thick round cake board
* about 2m pastel-pink satin ribbon, 15mm wide
* large serrated knife
* three 6 inch (15cm) thick round cake boards
* small kitchen knife
* pastry brush
* small and large palette knives
* large rolling pin
* ¼ inch (5mm) guide sticks
* 2 cake smoothers
* paper piping bags (see page 25)
* 3 small oasis dome flower holders
* three 4 inch (10cm) thin round cake boards
* scissors
* about 100 fresh roses in pastel yellow, peach and pink

1 At least 2 days ahead, colour your sugar paste: mix about 2kg with pink food colour, 1kg with orange and 500g yellow. Wrap separately in cling film until use.

2 Use about 500g of the pink paste to cover a 20 inch (50cm) cake board and then decorate the sides with pastel-pink satin ribbon as described on page 18. Let dry for at least 2 days.

3 Also at least 2 days ahead, trim the top crust of each sponge sheet using the serrated knife.

4 Using a 6 inch (15cm) round cake board as a template, lay it on top of the sponge sheet and cut three 6 inch (15cm) circles out of each sheet. (You will need 18 such circles in total.)

5 You will need 1 tier consisting of 3 sponge circles, 1 tier consisting of 6 sponge circles and 1 tier consisting of 9 sponge circles.

6 Using a pastry brush, soak the top of each tier with sugar syrup and, using a palette knife, fill each tier with the filling of your choice as described on page 16. Place each tier on a 6 inch (15cm) round cake board, fixing it in place with a dab of buttercream or chosen filling.

7 Cover all the cakes with marzipan as described on page 17 and let set for at least a day.

8 Next day, cover the cakes with sugar paste as described on page 17. Use the yellow paste for the small tier, the orange paste for the middle tier and the pink paste for the large tier. Let set for at least a day.

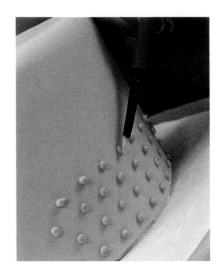

9 Once set, fill 3 paper piping bags with soft-peak royal icing of the same colour as the different sugar pastes and pipe small dots evenly all over the cakes. Should any of your dots form a peak, push it down with a damp brush while the icing is still wet, as shown above. Finish the top edge with a piped border of royal icing as described on page 25. Let the icing dry for a couple of hours.

10 Pipe some royal icing on top of the large iced cake board to make the cakes stick to the board and position the three iced cakes as centrally as possible on top, using the large palette knife.

11 Soak the oasis dome flower holders in water and place them on top of the cake with a thin 4 inch (10cm) round cake board under-neath to prevent the water from running on to the cake.

12 The flowers should stay fresh for up to 1 day, so if your wedding starts in the afternoon I would recommend you arrange the flowers no earlier than the late morning of the event. Cut the stems of each rose down to about 5cm from the head.

13 Stick the roses into the dome-shaped holders and lay some roses loosely on top of the cakes so that they are cascading from the top tier over the middle tier down to the bottom tier. Scatter some rose petals randomly over the cake board.

14 Remember to ensure that the flowers are removed from the cakes before they are cut and eaten.

gift box cake

If you are invited to a birthday party and you don't really know what to bring along, this cake is the ideal solution. Not only does it look like a genuine gift box, but the shimmering satin-like bow combined with the playful pink polka-dot design turns this simple cake into a funkily appealing present for people of all types and all ages. Make the bow at least 3 days ahead and the cake at least 2 days.

FOR AN 8 INCH (20CM) SQUARE CAKE (ABOUT 36 PORTIONS)

1.5kg white sugar paste

food colours (mint-green and pink)

1 tablespoon Tylo Powder

aqua shimmer powder

2 tablespoons clear alcohol, such as vodka

two 8 inch (20cm) square sponge cakes, using 1 recipe quantity of basic Victoria sponge mixture, flavoured to your choice (see page 12)

150ml sugar syrup (see page 15), flavoured to your choice

250g filling of your choice (butter cream, see page 14 or chocolate ganache, see page 15)

icing sugar for dusting

750g white marzipan

small amount of stiff-peak royal icing (see page 24)

EQUIPMENT

* cling film
* small rolling pin
* small plastic board
* small kitchen knife
* thick soft artist's brush
* tissue paper
* greaseproof paper
* 8 inch (20cm) square cake board
* serrated knife
* pastry brush
* large palette knife
* ¼ inch (5mm) guide sticks
* large rolling pin
* 2 cake smoothers
* selection of small round cutters in various sizes
* paper piping bag (see page 25)

Start by making the loop for the sugar bow at least 3 days ahead

1 Mix about 500g of the white sugar paste with a little bit of mint-green food colour until the paste is a light green in colour. Knead the Tylo Powder into the paste (it is a hardening agent and will make the paste more flexible and stable), wrap it in cling film and let it rest for about half an hour.

2 Once rested, take a piece of the paste and you will feel how the paste has become a lot more flexible for moulding and shaping. Using a small rolling pin, roll a piece of paste out on a plastic board until very thin. Using a small sharp knife, cut a strip about 2 x 6 inches (5 x 15cm) out of the paste.

3 Remove the trimmings and dust the strip with the aqua shimmer, using a thick soft artist's brush (see 1 overleaf).

4 Turn the strip upside-down (see 2). Roll up some tissue paper into a cylinder about 2 inches (5cm) in diameter, place it in the middle of the strip of paste and wrap the paste around it as shown (see 3). Pinch both ends together, using a little bit of water or alcohol to make them stick. Transfer to a piece of greaseproof paper. Repeat this procedure again for the other half of the bow. Let both dry for at least 3 days.

PREPARE THE SPONGE CAKES:

5 Trim the top crust of both sponges, using the serrated knife. Soak them with sugar syrup and layer both with your chosen filling, as described on page 16.

6 Coat the outside of the cake with the same filling and chill for at least 2 hours.

7 Once chilled, take the cake out of the fridge, place it on top of an 8 inch (20cm) cake board and give it another coat of ganache or buttercream to make the marzipan stick to the cake.

8 On a surface dusted with icing sugar, roll out the marzipan between ¼ inch (5mm) guide sticks using a large rolling pin.

9 Lay the marzipan over the top of the cake and push down the side. Trim away excess marzipan with a knife. Use the cake smoothers to make the top and sides nice and even.

10 Brush the outside of the marzipanned cake with a little bit of alcohol to make the sugar paste stick to the marzipan.

11 Cover the cake with 900g sugar paste following the same technique as for the marzipan. Let set overnight.

DECORATE THE CAKE:

12 Roll out the leftover green sugar paste for the bow and cut out 2 long strips of the same width as the bow and long enough to reach from one side of the cake to the other.

13 Dust each strip with the aqua shimmer as before (see 1). Using alcohol to stick the paste to the

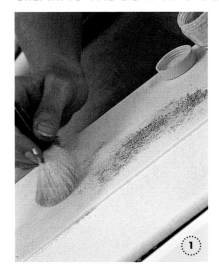

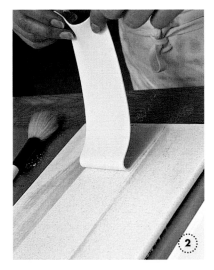

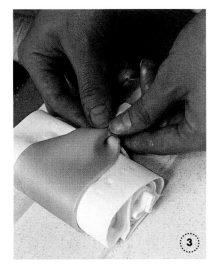

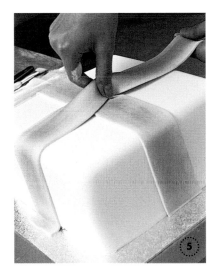

cake, lay the green sugar paste strips across and over the cake and pinch both strips together where they meet at the top of the cake (see 4 and 5). Trim the excess paste at the sides using a small knife.

14 Colour half of the remaining white sugar paste pale pink and the other half bright pink.

15 Roll the paste out on a small plastic board and cut out circles in different sizes using round cutters.

16 Arrange these randomly on the white parts of the cake (see 6), using some clear alcohol or water to make them stick.

17 Place the bow on top of the cake and fix it with a dab of royal icing.

18 For the end pieces of the bow, roll out another piece of paste as before and cut out 2 strips about 2 x 5 inches (5 x 12cm). Cut a 'V' into one end of each and pinch the other ends together. Stick to the

bow with royal icing and lay them on top of the cake in a wavy shape.

19 Finally, roll out another small piece of green paste, dust with shimmer and wrap it around the middle of the bow.

pink wedding cake

This gorgeous and girly creation of pastel-pink icing and white hydrangea sugar blossoms will help give any wedding that 'fairytale come true' feeling. Make this cake at least 3 days in advance. For an even more magical effect, you can sprinkle the white blossom with some white edible glitter while it is still wet.

FOR ABOUT 130 PORTIONS

5kg pastel-pink sugar paste

two 6 inch (15cm) round sponge cakes, each using ½ recipe quantity of basic Victoria sponge mixture, flavoured to your choice (see page 12)

two 8 inch (20cm) round sponge cakes, each using ⅔ recipe quantity of basic Victoria sponge mixture, flavoured to your choice (see page 12)

two 10 inch (25cm) round sponge cakes, each using ¾ recipe quantity of basic Victoria sponge mixture, flavoured to your choice (see page 12)

two 12 inch (30cm) round sponge cakes, each using 1 recipe quantity of basic Victoria sponge mixture, flavoured to your choice (see page 12)

700ml sugar syrup (see page 15), flavoured to your choice

2kg buttercream (see page 14) or other filling of your choice

5kg marzipan

icing sugar for dusting

1kg royal icing (see page 24) for making the flowers

pink food colour

EQUIPMENT

✳ 16 inch (40cm) round cake board

✳ large serrated knife

✳ pastry brush

✳ large palette knife

✳ about 4m white satin ribbon, 15mm wide

✳ 6 inch (15cm) thin round cake board

✳ 8 inch (20cm) thin round cake board

✳ 10 inch (25cm) thin round cake board

✳ 12 inch (30cm) thin round cake board

✳ large rolling pin

✳ ¼ inch (5mm) guide sticks

✳ 2 cake smoothers

✳ paper piping bags (see page 25)

✳ piping nozzles (Wilton 103, PME, etc.)

✳ flower nail

✳ greaseproof paper

✳ turntable

✳ 12 plastic dowels

1 Cover a 16 inch (40cm) cake board with 350g pink sugar paste (see page 17. Cover sides with white ribbon.

2 You'll need 4 cake tiers, each consisting of 2 layered sponges (see above). Trim, soak and fill each tier as on page 16, then set it on an appropriate thin cake board. Chill.

3 Cover each tier with marzipan as on page 17. Let set overnight.

4 Pipe the hydrangea blossoms in different sizes using stiff royal icing. Make as 5-petal flowers (see page 26), but only pipe 4 petals. Mix a little of the icing with pink food colour and pipe the stamens in the centres. Let dry overnight.

5 Next day, cover each cake with pink sugar paste as on page 17. Let it set for one more night.

6 Once set, assemble the tiers and the cake board on top of each other as described on page 19.

7 Arrange ribbon around base of each tier. Stick flowers along the sides of each with stiff royal icing.

English rose wedding cake

I recently saw a wallpaper design by Cath Kidston in an interiors magazine which has inspired this cake. I simply love the old-fashioned effect, it's so beautifully British and makes me think of English rose gardens. The technique used for painting the flowers on the cake is called 'brush embroidery'. If you haven't done this before, you might find it a bit difficult at the beginning, so I suggest you try it out on a cake board iced with sugar paste first until you are happy with the results, before you start with the cake. Make this cake at least 3 days in advance.

FOR 110 PORTIONS

3.5kg white sugar paste

food colours (pink, yellow and green)

two 6 inch (15cm) round sponge cakes, each using ½ recipe quantity of basic Victoria sponge mixture, flavoured to your choice (see page 12)

two 9 inch (23cm) round sponge cakes, each using ¾ recipe quantity of basic Victoria sponge mixture, flavoured to your choice (see page 12)

two 12 inch (30cm) round sponge cakes, using 1 recipe quantity of basic Victoria sponge mixture, flavoured to your choice (see page 12)

500ml sugar syrup (see page 15), flavoured to your choice

1.5 kg buttercream (see page 14) or other filling of your choice

icing sugar for dusting

3kg white marzipan

500g royal icing (see page 24)

EQUIPMENT

* about 1.5m bright pink satin ribbon, 30mm wide
* about 1.5m bright pink satin ribbon, 15mm wide
* one 16 inch (40cm) thick round cake board
* 1 thin 6 inch (15cm) round cake board
* 1 thin 9 inch (23cm) round cake board
* 1 thin 12 inch (30cm) round cake board
* large serrated knife
* pastry brush
* large palette knife
* large rolling pin
* ¼ inch (5mm) guide sticks
* 2 cake smoothers
* rose and rose leaf embossers
* paper piping bags (see page 25)
* fine artist's brush
* turntable
* two thick 3 inch (7cm) round cake boards
* two thick 6 inch (15cm) round cake boards
* two thick 9 inch (23cm) round cake boards
* needles
* 8 plastic dowels
* scissors

1 Mix about 350g of white sugar paste with pink food colour until it has a deep fuchsia-pink colour, similar to that of the ribbon you are using. Use this paste to cover a 16 inch (40cm) thick round cake board as described on page 18. Cover the sides of the board with the 15mm wide satin ribbon.

2 You will need 3 cake tiers, each consisting of 3 layered sponges, one 6 inches (15cm) round, one 9 inches (23cm) round and one 12 inches (30cm) round. Trim, soak and fill each tier as described on page 16, then set it on an appropriate thin cake board.

3 Cover each cake with marzipan as described on page 18 and let it set overnight.

4 Before covering the cakes with sugar paste, have rose and rose leaf embossers ready. Cover one cake with white sugar paste at a time, as described on page 17.

5 While the paste is still soft, push the embossers carefully into the paste of one cake to create an all-over rose and leaf design (see 1). Repeat for the other cakes and leave them to dry overnight.

6 Colour your royal icing and prepare your icing bags. You will need several piping bags filled with soft-peak royal icing in each of the following colours: fuchsia pink, pastel pink, green and yellow.

7 Start with the green leaves: pipe the outline of the leaf shape using the green icing. Take a fine artist's brush and dampen it with water. Use the brush to pull the icing from the outside into the middle of the leaf (see 2), which will create the veins of the leaves. Repeat for all the leaves, cleaning your brush from time to time.

8 When finished with the leaves, pipe the pink flowers: pipe each rose a petal at a time. Pipe one line of fuchsia-pink icing on the outline of a petal and pipe another line of pastel-pink icing next to it on the inside of the petal (see 3). Take the damp artist's brush and pull it from the outside edge to the centre of the flowers so that the two pink colours blend together. Repeat for all the rose petals, cleaning your brush from time to time.

9 To pipe the centres: take the yellow icing and pipe little dots into the middle of each open rose (see 4). Let dry for an hour or two.

10 Place one tier at a time on a turntable and, using a piping bag filled with white soft-peak royal icing, pipe a border along bottom and top edge of each tier. Let dry.

11 Stick two 3 inch (7.5cm) thick round cake boards together with a dab of royal icing. Do the same with two 6 inch (15cm) thick round cake boards and two 9 inch (23cm) thick round cake boards. These will form the cake separators.

12 Cover the sides of each separator with 30mm wide satin ribbon and fix with a pin as on page 18.

13 Now assemble the whole cake. Mark 4 points in the middle of the bottom tier so that they form a 5 inch (12.5cm) square. Stick 4 plastic dowels into the cake at these points and cut them to the right length as described on page 19.

14 Repeat for the second tier, positioning the dowels in the middle to form a 2 inch (5cm) square.

15 Stick the 9 inch (23cm) round separator in the centre of the iced 16 inch (40cm) thick round cake board, using a dab of royal icing. Centre the 12 inch (30cm) bottom tier on top.

16 Place the 6 inch (15cm) round cake separator on the bottom tier so it covers the plastic dowels that are stuck inside the bottom tier.

17 Next, place the 9 inch (23cm) middle tier on top, followed by the 3 inch (7.5cm) round separator and finally the 6 inch (15cm) top tier.

'makes me think of English rose gardens'

dropping daisies

Rather similar in concept to the earlier Pink Wedding Cake, this equally striking cake is made just that touch more playful by the addition of the white sugar bows and by the use of a refreshing mint green as the base colour.

FOR ABOUT 90 PORTIONS

500g stiff-peak royal icing (see page 24)

yellow food colour

icing sugar for dusting

small amount of clear alcohol (such as vodka) or water

250g white sugar paste

filled and iced cake as described on pages 16–17

EQUIPMENT

* metal piping nozzle Wilton 104 /103
* greaseproof paper
* flower nail
* paper piping bags (see page 25)
* small rolling pin
* fine artist's brush
* small plastic board
* small kitchen knife

1 Using white and yellow stiff-peak royal icing, paper piping bags and piping nozzles, pipe 120 sugar daisies as described on page 27 in 3 different sizes. Let dry overnight.

2 Meanwhile, on a surface dusted with icing sugar, roll the white sugar paste out to a long strip and cut out two ¾ inch (2cm) wide strips that are long enough to go around the sides of the cakes.

3 Brush the bottom edge of each tier with alcohol or water using an artist's brush, and stick the strips of paste around each tier (see 1). Make sure you start and finish in the centre of the same side.

4 To make the bows, roll a smaller piece of paste out on the small plastic board and cut out two strips ¾ inch (2cm) wide and 5 inches (12cm) in length.

5 Using a small kitchen knife, cut two 'V' shapes out of the middle of each strip opposite each other (see 2).

6 Brush the middle of each strip with a little bit of water or alcohol and bring both ends of each strip to the middle to form the bow (see 3).

7 Roll another small amount of paste out and cut out 2 pieces of about ½ x ¾ inch (1 x 2cm). Brush the middle of each bow with some water or alcohol and push one small piece of the cut-out paste into the centre of each bow.

8 Stick each bow on to the sides of each tier where the ends of the paste strips join together, fixing it in place with some water or alcohol. Open up the bow's loops slightly to give them shape.

9 Finally stick the daisies randomly along the top edge of each tier, using dabs of royal icing.

romantic rose tower

Voluptuous roses in luscious pinks and gorgeous butterflies 'fluttering' at the end of curled wires turn this cake into a piece of pure romance. Inspired by *A Midsummer Night's Dream*, I designed this cake to create something different and unusual as a glamorous centrepiece for wedding receptions and birthday parties. It is very time-consuming to make, but is well worth the effort. You can make the roses a few weeks in advance, as they will keep well.

FOR 120 PARTY PORTIONS:

You need to do this at least 3 days ahead and make your marzipan roses and leaves at least 24 hours in advance to ensure they are dry.

4 sheets of Chocolate Sponge (see page 12)

1 recipe quantity Chocolate Ganache
(see page 15)

icing sugar for dusting

2kg marzipan

2kg pink sugar paste

a little clear alcohol, such as
vodka or gin

about 120 Marzipan Roses (see page 29) in different shades of pink about 24 Marzipan Rose Leaves (page 29)

pink Royal Icing (page 24)

EQUIPMENT

* about 10 round templates with diameters from 2 to 12 inches (5cm to 30cm) for cutting out the cake layers
* 12 inch (30cm) round cake board
* large palette knife
* large rolling pin
* ¼ inch (5mm) guide sticks
* small kitchen knife
* pastry brush
* paper piping bag (see page 25)
* 16 + 18 inch (40cm + 45cm) round double cake board covered with pale pink sugar paste and deep pink ribbon (see page 18)
* wired feather butterflies (see Suppliers, page 142)

1 Using your templates, cut out rounds of sponge with diameters graduated from 2 inches to 12 inches (5cm to 30cm).

2 Using a large palette knife, spread a small amount of ganache on a 12 inch (30cm) cake board and place the 12 inch (30cm) sponge on top. Spread a thin layer of ganache over this first layer and place the next-largest sponge on top. Continue to assemble the cake layer by layer in this way to form a cone shape.

'this cake is pure romance'

3 Cover the whole cake with chocolate ganache and smooth the surface. Place the cake in the fridge and leave it to set for at least 2 hours.

4 Dust your working surface with icing sugar and roll out the marzipan to a thickness of ¼ inch (5mm), using your guide sticks. Make a paper template that will be big enough to form a cone, when rolled, that will cover the cake. Use this to mark and cut out a triangle of marzipan large enough to cover the cake.

5 Apply another thin coat of ganache to the cake.

6 Use your rolling pin to lift the marzipan triangle and carefully wrap it around the cake. Trim off excess top and the bottom. Leave it to harden overnight.

7 Next day, following the same procedure as with the marzipan, cover the cake with pink sugar paste, but instead of using chocolate ganache to stick it on, first brush the cake with the alcohol. Let the paste harden overnight.

8 Next day, pipe a dot of icing in the centre of the double cake board and place the cake on top.

9 Decorate the cake by sticking the marzipan roses and leaves on it with pink royal icing, starting at the bottom and working your way upwards (see 1 and 2 above).

10 Finally, stick the wired butterflies into the marzipan roses evenly over the cake, using larger butterflies at the bottom and smaller ones at the top.

11 When serving, make everyone aware that the wired butterflies are not edible, and make sure that they are removed before the cutting and eating of the cake.

templates ﹏﹏﹏﹏﹏﹏﹏﹏﹏﹏﹏﹏﹏﹏﹏﹏﹏﹏﹏﹏﹏

For reasons of space I haven't tried to supply templates for every project. You should usually be able to find appropriate cutters or make your own templates if you need to. Here, though, are templates for the two projects where they are really necessary (you have to pipe directly on to a template) – the Christmas Trees on pages 72–3 and the Butterfly Fancies on pages 76–9.

glossary

Most items listed here are available from specialist suppliers (opposite) although some of the more everyday ones can be found in supermarkets and cookware shops.

Ingredients

FONDANT Made from sugar, water and cream of tartar, fondant is widely used as a glaze in confectionery as well as in pâtisserie and cake-decorating. Ready-made fondant is available from specialist suppliers or from supermarkets as a powder to be mixed with water.

FOOD COLOURS The food colours used in this book are those in either liquid or paste form. The pastes are more concentrated than the liquids and therefore more useful for colouring sugar pastes and marzipans. Liquid colours mix faster and give more even results with royal icing.

GLITTER, EDIBLE Make sure it is edible and not simply non-toxic.

GLUCOSE, LIQUID This is a thick version of corn syrup used to make fondant icing in order to give it a beautiful shine.

LUSTER, EDIBLE This non-toxic pearl dust comes in different shades. Edible luster can either be mixed to a thick paste with a drop of alcohol or it can be applied directly with a soft artist's brush.

MARZIPAN Made from ground almonds and icing sugar, marzipan is mainly used for covering large cakes before icing them, as it seals in moisture as well as helping to stabilize shape. Also, marzipan is ideal for making marzipan flowers (see pages 28–9), as it is very easy to mould and the individual petals stick to each other naturally.

MERRIWHITE This is dried egg white powder used instead of fresh egg whites in making royal icing for food safety reasons, as the dried egg white is pasteurized.

ROYAL ICING This decorative icing, made of icing sugar and egg white or dried egg white (merriwhite, see above), dries very hard and white, and can be easily tinted with food colouring.

SUGAR PASTE A very smooth and pliable icing made from gelatin, icing sugar and water, which dries hard. Sugar paste is used for covering cakes and for making flowers and modelling cake decorations.

TYLO POWDER If mixed into sugar paste, marzipan or royal icing, this harmless chemical, carboxymethycellulose (CMC), will form a strong modelling paste that dries hard. Tylo powder can also be mixed with a bit of water to make a thick and strong edible glue.

Equipment

BONE TOOL A long plastic stick with two rounded ends that looks almost like a bone, a bone tool is used for shaping the petals of sugar paste flowers.

CAKE SMOOTHERS For icing cakes, you always need at least two of these. Cake smoothers are flat rectangular pieces of smooth plastic, with a handle, that are used to smoothe the marzipan and sugar paste icing on a cake.

CEL STICK This is a thin plastic stick for shaping flowers.

DOWELS, PLASTIC These long sturdy plastic sticks, which can be cut to the required size are used to support the top tiers in large cakes.

FOAM PAD A foam pad is used as a yielding surface for thinning the edges of flower paste with a bone tool (see above).

FLOWER CUTTERS Made of metal or plastic, flower cutters are used to cut petals and leaves out of flower paste. In this book I have used cutters to make sugar pansies, daisies and mini blossoms.

FLOWER NAIL A stainless steel flower nail is used for making royal icing sugar flowers. It functions as a convenient supporting base for the piping of daisies, pansies, daffodils, etc. as it may be turned readily in the non-piping hand.

GUIDE STICKS These long plastic sticks of are used to roll out dough or sugar paste to an even thickness, usually ¼ inch (5mm).

LEAF VEINER/VEINING MAT A rubber mat used for shaping and marking leaves made of flower paste or marzipan.

PALETTE KNIFE A broad-bladed long flat knife without a sharp edge for use in spreading cream and other fillings. The step palette knife has an angled blade that makes it useful for lifting large cakes.

PIPING NOZZLES Stainless steel piping nozzles are used for piping flowers and leaves from royal icing. They are available in different shapes and sizes. My favourite brands are Wilton and PME.

ROSE AND LEAF EMBOSSER Usually made of plastic, embossers are used to push the impression of a pattern into icing. In this book I have used rose and leaf embossers to create the design for my English Rose Wedding Cake (see page 130–3), which I afterwards painted over with a technique called brush embroidery.

ROSE CALYX CUTTER These metal or plastic cutters are used for cutting the calyx for a rose out of flower paste or marzipan.

ROSE PUSH-IN MOULD A flexible rubber mould for shaping roses out of sugar paste that is easy to use by simply pushing the paste into the mould. The sugar rose is then released by turning the mould inside out.

SIDE SCRAPER Best made of stainless steel, a side scraper is a flat piece of metal with a straight side that is used for scraping the excess cream off the side of a cake when filling it. It will help give perfectly straight sides to your cake.

suppliers

UK

For general cake decorating tools and equipment:

Jane Asher Party Cakes
24 Cale Street
London SW3 3QU
www.jane-asher.co.uk

Squires Kitchen
Squires House
3 Waverley Lane
Farnham, Surrey
GU9 8BB
www.squires-group.co.uk

The Sugar Shack
Unit D1
Phoenix Industrial Estate
Rosslyn Crescent
Harrow, Middlesex
HA1 2SP
www.sugarshack.co.uk

For general cake decorating tools, equipment and luster powder:

Almond Art
Unit 15 & 16
Faraday Close
Gorse Lane Industrial Estate
Clacton-on-Sea, Essex
CO15 4TR
www.almondart.com

For feather butterflies (see the Romantic Rose Tower on pages 136–9) & Ribbons:

V V Rouleaux
54 Sloane Square
London SW1W 8AX
www.vvrouleaux.com

GERMANY

For general cake decorating tools and equipment:

Kopyform GmbH
Rufdolf-Diesel-Straße 1
67259 Beindersheim
www.kopyform.de

Robert Oppeneder
St.-Martin-Straße 38
81541 München
www.sweetart.de

BENELUX

For general cake decorating tools, equipment:

Ranson NV,
Gen. Deprezstraat 16
Harelbeke
Belgium

USA

For general cake decorating tools and equipment:

Sugarcraft, Inc.
2715 Dixie Hwy.
Hamilton, Ohio 45015
www.sugarcraft.com

For cookie cutters:

Kitchen Collectables, Inc.
8901 J Street
Suite 2
Omaha
Nebraska 68127
www.kitchengifts.com

CopperGifts.com
900 N. 32nd St.
Parsons
KS 67357
www.coppergifts.com

acknowledgements

Although I've been lucky enough to be making cakes for a lot of high-profile clients right from the start, I have always considered myself as quite a freshman in the cake decorating business. Writing a book has always been one of my goals for later, but I'd have never thought that this dream would come true so soon. I would like especially to thank Katrin Cargill, who got the ball rolling. She found me at a Christmas fair in Chelsea last year and introduced me to Jane O'Shea and Helen Lewis from Quadrille.

Jane and Helen, I would like to thank you both for giving me this amazing opportunity and for providing such an enjoyable and inspirational working atmosphere. I was given the most fantastic team of very inspiring people to create this book. I would like to thank my photographer, the gorgeous Georgia Glynn Smith for taking the most beautiful images of my cakes. I think you've brought the best out of them. Thank you Chalkley Calderwood Pratt for designing this book, I love your style and I think you're fabulous.

Writing this book has proven to be a lot more difficult for me than making the cakes and cookies. This is where I would like to thank my editor Lewis Esson, for giving me a lot of advice and for adding charm and flair to this book.

Last but not least, I would like to say my biggest thank you to my wonderful partner, Bryn, who has been my rock throughout this whole project. Without your devotion, none of this would have been possible.